GLOBALIZATION Public Administration Essays

GLOBALIZATION Public Administration Essays

Budget * Sexual Harassment * Internet * Impeachment * Finance * Communication * Bureaucracy

Rony Curvelo

Writers Club Press
San Jose New York Lincoln Shanghai

GLOBALIZATION Public Administration Essays
Budget * Sexual Harassment * Internet * Impeachment * Finance *
Communication * Bureaucracy

Writers Club Press
an imprint of iUniverse.com, Inc.

For information address:
iUniverse.com, Inc.
5220 S 16th, Ste. 200
Lincoln, NE 68512
www.iuniverse.com

ISBN: 0-595-16829-9

Printed in the United States of America

To my lovely wife Maria Helena, my son Ronnie and my daughter Jennifer.

Contents

List of Abbreviations

Regulatory Agencies

BLS   Bureau of Labor Statistic
CEA   Council of Economic Advisors
CFTC   Commodity Futures Trading Commission.
CAB   Civil Aeronautics Board
CPSC   Consumer Product Safety Commission
DOD   Department of Defense
DOT   Department of Transportation
EEOC   Equal Employment Opportunity Commission
EPA   Environmental Protection Agency
FAA   Federal Aviation Administration
FAO   Food and Agricultural Organization
FCC   Federal Communication Commission
FDA   Federal and Drug Administration
FDIC   Federal Deposit Insurance Corporation
FEC   FederalElection Commission
FERC   Federal Energy Regulatory Commission
FHA   Federal Housing Administration
FMC   Federal Maritime Commission
FSLIC   Federal saviings and Loan Insurance Corporation
FTC   Federal trade Commission
ICC   Interstate Commerce Commission
ITC   International Trade Commission
NHTSA   National Highway Traffic Safety Administration
NIH   National Institute of Health

NIOSH   National Institute of Occupational Safety and Health
NLRB   National Labor Relations Board
NRC   National Regulatory Commission
OIRA   Office of Informationand Regulatory Affairs
OMB   Office of Management and Budget
OSHA   Occupational Safety and Health Administration
SEC   Securities and Exchange Commission
USDA   United States Department of Agriculture

Chapter 1

Internet:
The Dictator's New Enemy

The Internet has grown at a pace that no one would have believed possible. In numbers of service providers alone (such as America Online, Earthlink, etc.), there were *213* in 1981, *1,000* in 1984, *100,000* in 1989, *a million* in 1992 and *9.5 million* in 1996. Between mid-1995 and mid-1996, *five million* servers were created.

Internet content has also changed as dramatically as its size. Many individuals remain in uproar over the pornographic material available over the Internet, but scientific information abounds, as does business information, stock trading and information on every topic imaginable.

However, the Internet, the outcome of a successful marriage between telecommunications and information technology, is posing unprecedented information control problems which governments, service providers, educators and families are finding hard to solve.

An uncensored Net connection can be as deadly to a 21th century government as the plague was three centuries ago. But the infection cyberspace spreads today is far more virulent than even the bubonic plague. Anathema to government, the Net carries the virus of freedom.

That proliferation of information of all types is precisely what non-democratic governments fear. Those repressive governments are concerned with the free dissemination of political ideas that do not match their own agendas. All nations with unrestricted Internet access are concerned with the moral aspects of much of the information available, specially when the very nature of the Internet is conducive to anonymity, making it the ideal medium to use "for subversive ends and as an alternative to censored traditional media".

Newspapers, television and radio stations, and news services maintain physical locations and have specific transmittal sites that must be operational for their messages to get through to someone else. Because the traditional media are so identifiable and are limited to physical locations, restrictive governments are free to close them down should their information become objectionable to the government. In addition, it is common for the most restrictive of governments to own and operate all media sources within their respective nations.

Introducing the Internet into the scenario changes all the rules under which governments and their people alike had been accustomed to operating rather than relative few transmitters of information, there are innumerable such transmitters with the Internet. More than 100 million people have access to the Internet, and a relatively high percentage of them would be capable of turning their own computers into service providers of sorts. Afterward, his or her message can travel along so many routes that when it reaches its destination, the original source can no longer be traced. This lack of identifiability makes it doubly difficult for restrictive governments to fully control the information both entering and leaving their countries when the Internet is involved.

Some countries

Many nations of the world have widely divergent views of what is and what is not acceptable to be contained within the Internet. *Reporters sans Frontieres* (RsF) is a French-based group monitoring governmental views of Internet access and use within their respective countries. Recently, the group named 45 countries as being *enemies* of the Internet, 20 of which can be considered to be the worst in the world in terms of allowing Internet access to their citizens. Those *worst* are: the countries of Central Asia and the Caucasus (Azerbaijan, Kazakhstan, Kirghizia, Tajikistan, Turkmenistan and Uzbekistan), Belarus, Burma, China, Cuba, Iran, Iraq, Libya, North Korea, Saudi Arabia, Sierra Leone, Sudan, Syria, Tunisia and Vietnam.

Filtering Internet information with the intention of blocking the most objectionable of Websites also comes under fire from the RsF. "…medical students in Iran are unable to access Websites dealing with anatomy and surfing via any of Saudi Arabia's private ISPs run through government filters that seek to maintain Islamic values" , said Martyn William in the latest edition of RsF.

The situation is much different in some other nations, however. An Example is Burma, where Internet access is allowed only through the government-run service provider. There, computer owners must register their equipment with the government or face a 15-year jail term if discovered. Registration is more difficult in some other countries. Restrictions in Vietnam mean all Internet use has to be approved by the government through permits from the interior ministry and access via state-run ISPs.

It is fairly common to find nations that do not allow their citizens free and unrestricted access to the information contained within the Internet, but identical end results can stem from several different types of motivations. As example, Cuba and China seek to maintain control over the people of those nations, for the good of the government rather than for the good of the people. Singapore, however, appears to have different intentions though they achieve the same results. The people of the nation are prevented full access to the Internet, but it at least is done in Singapore with the spirit of *protecting* the population.

Singapore

Singapore has long been derided by much of the rest of the world for its protectionist views of the people of the nation. Singapore led the entire region of Southeast Asia in industrialization and attainment of prosperity for many years before the advent of the Asian currency crisis and the near-insolvency of Malaysia threatened to destroy the interdependent economies of ASEAN, the Association of Southeast Asian Nations.

When the government began its plan for pursuing prosperity in the 1960s, it took diverse steps to protect the people. By the 1990s, Singapore citizens were not allowed to work a full 40-hour work week, and they were encouraged to save to buy their own homes. Shortly before the beginning of the Asian currency crisis, Singapore's gross domestic product had surpassed that of Great Britain after nearly a decade of economic expansion in double digits. The government requires that each working citizen save a percentage of income for retirement. Singapore remained far more fiscally conservative than their other ASEAN counterparts, with the result that the Singapore dollar lost only a fraction of its value during the currency crisis while its neighbors' currencies became all but worthless. The stability of the economy in the face of such crisis served to quiet most of the criticism in economic matters.

Education is a primary and united goal, one that both the people and the government take seriously as the key to continued economic success.

Education in academic basics is paramount, but the people of Singapore are quite comfortable with the electronic devices that contain the semiconductors that raised the nation from Third World to middle-income developed. School children have the option of supplementing their in-class instruction with a government-supported and Internet-based tutoring system that is open not only to citizens of Singapore, but to any student in the world.

Internet access in Singapore is a matter of choice. All service providers within the country are accountable to the government for the content they provide their customers, and the government has issued strict rules by which libraries and schools will guard the information gained through their Internet connections. In 1996, the government ordered that internet providers censor materials on sex, religion, and politics. New rules require libraries, schools, cybercafes, and other access sites to supervise Internet use. Newspaper reports indicate that there are about 100,000 users in Singapore, where restricting books, movies, and political activity is a long-standing practice.

Unlike other nations, however, Singapore citizens and other residents have the option of using access services outside the country. Of course that access is for a price, which equates to per-minute international telephone charges. Any service provider located within the country is subject to Singapore laws.

Some people calls Singapore's Internet policies *reprehensible* and states that the government, "a critic of unfettered dissent and Western culture, is trying to become the network's model censor". In those terms, it would appear that Singapore's only reason for censorship of the Internet within the nation is that of maintaining absolute control over its citizens. Their methods may be questionable in the eyes of the rest of the portion of the world that allows unlimited access, but motives are far more pure than those of nations such as China or Cuba.

Cuba

A primary distinguishing difference between Singapore and Cuba is that Singapore prefers to keep its people productive, supporting themselves, prospering and not looking to the government to supply their every need. Cuba's history under Castro has been that the dictator maintains absolute control over the people of the nation. Though Fidel Castro has changed his economic attitudes in recent years as he reaches to democratic nations to help grow Cuba's people out of their abject poverty, his, and therefore Cuba's, ideologies have remained constant. There will be control of all aspects of Cuban citizens' lives.

The French RsF monitors the fate of independent journalists in Cuba. The group continually petition the government to cease harassment of journalists and to free those that have been imprisoned, but Cuba is still trying and convicting any who present views inconsistent with official government position. Currently, there are at least three journalists imprisoned in Cuba. The most recently convicted has been Jesus Diaz Hernandez of the Cooperative of Independent Journalists, imprisoned in June 1999. He was sentenced to four years imprisonment after being convicted of posing a social threat—a charge sometimes used against dissidents in Cuba. The sentence of one of the three has not yet begun, though it is rather assured that there will be trial and conviction forthcoming. Manuel Gonzalez already has been held for three months without trial.

The charges are all the same, however. These independent journalists *work* in Cuba, generally sending reports abroad for use on the Internet. They are considered dissidents by the government which often denounces them as *counter-revolutionaries* in the pay of the United States.

Granma, the official newspaper of Cuba's ruling communist party, announced In 1996 that Internet access would be allowed in Cuba, but would be restricted to those individuals and bodies with most relevance to the country's life and development. The information available would be kept to interests of defense and national security, and would be maintained according to Cuba's ethical principles. A committee regulating the policy on global information networks would be drawn from ministries that will include the Interior Ministry, the Justice Ministry and the Armed Forces Ministry.

China

The China of the 1990s presents the perfect study in paradox. After witnessing the growing prosperity of its neighbors that were participating in the emerging global market, China began opening its borders to increasing numbers of Western nations after the death of Chairman Mao. The government understood that it could not continue its isolationist policies and simultaneously be a significant factor on the world stage, and it could not alone provide sustenance for the world's largest national population. China's openness to foreign direct investment is bringing electrification and telecommunication to regions of the nation that had not been able to have even the benefit of electricity. Multinational enterprises establishing new plants in China now are prevented from locating in the prosperous Southeast coastal region where the Chinese government began its economic experiment, and are required to locate in remote areas, supplying their own supportive infrastructure such as roads and power.

China is a modern study in contrasts, containing within its borders some of the most modern of cities and also some of the most basic of villages. Clearly, Internet usage is not available to all citizens. Those with access to computers in areas where they are useable machines are required to pledge non-subversiveness to the government and are required to register with the police and agree not to use the medium for "antigovernment activities. What's more, the government, which has every modern-owner on file, has monitored all traffic since 1996. By 1998, the government had made it illegal to use the Internet to obtain stock market information that could be considered strategic.

Clearly, China's regulation of Internet usage is open to being highly subjective when it is based on *considerations* of information rather than on specific content. Because of its subjectivity, regulations can be read to mean nearly anything at any time. The government was speaking of expanding service several years ago, yet retaining close restrictions on use. The plan in 1996 was to develop an intranet that would allow access only to those sites that the government deemed appropriate, but users were not confident that the government could attain the level of control that it sought The ultimate goal of such an approach was to allow *unlimited* access for Chinese users to each other, but highly restricted access to the outside world.

The French RsF strongly condemns China for its Internet policies, even though Internet usage has been increasing rapidly. The group cited in its condemnation the case of Lin Hai, a computer technician who was jailed for supplying Chinese e-mail addresses to a US-based dissident site that publishes an e-mail newsletter critical of the government, and the June closure of 300 unlicensed cybercafes in Shanghai. RsF also listed in its reasons for its condemnation of China the government's practice of periodically blocking the sites of organizations it sees as dissident, or those carrying international news. BBC Online and New Century Net are common targets for disruption on the part of the Chinese government.

Though Singapore's approach to limiting Internet access is much more benevolent than that of China, one government official said that China has a lot to learn from Singapore's experience. In the face of increasing threat that Internet access could undermine the Chinese communist message, the Chinese instituted controls in 1996 that were much stronger than any then to date. The government appeared to be concerned that messages of democracy from the outside world would be used by Chinese dissidents to dilute the powers of the communist government.

In an effort to bring more useable Internet-based information into China, a state-instituted venture created a server that permitted access only to business-related information. The network was 60 percent owned by the government and carried no questionable content so that it would better withstand scrutiny for possible illegalities.

Other Manifestations

China, Cuba and Singapore all have service providers located within their borders, all of which must adhere to the censorship laws of their respective countries. There are many other nations that have Internet access available, but no servers are located within their borders. As example, Iraq has limited Internet access, but all servers for Iraq are located in Jordan .

Constant monitoring of Internet activity and usage is more difficult when access comes from outside the nation. In Algeria, Internet users have access to a site created by *dissident officers* in the armed forces. "The Algerian government doesn't like our site's content....We use the Web as an opportunity," says the site's anonymous webmaster. Citizens of censoring nations can still use the Internet to disseminate their anti-governmental messages, though they generally must be outside their native countries.

Today, opponents of monolithic regimes can use the Internet to set up areas of freedom that are forbidden in their own countries and can reach an international audience that would be difficult to obtain otherwise. Censors around the world are coming up against this phenomenon because "right now the Internet is the only area of freedom outside all political control," says Lyonnel Thouvenot of Reporters without Frontiers.

Some observers note that few nations have laws specifically targeting the Internet. Everything depends on how existing laws on freedom of expression are applied, on the margin of manoeuvre [sic] one has to criticize the government, on the national definitions of content that could endanger state security.

So far full censorship is not possible, the primary route that restrictive governments take to achieve the levels of censorship that they do is that of encryption technology. Censoring nations maintain control of encryption processes, which they must control in order to control the types of information that are allowed to come within their borders. In fact, every state fears that these massive, repeated, cross-border electronic exchanges, which escape all control, will limit their powers and privileges in the age of globalization. Most experts agree that the Internet must move out of its present primitive stage, in which scholars and *plugged-in* individuals exchange information, and become an instrument of mass commercial communication, whether it is used by companies between themselves, by producers, or by consumers.

Final

The American Civil Liberties Union (ACLU) and the Electronic Frontier Foundation (EFF) continue to fight for an end to censorship on the Internet, but it remains unlikely that the worst offenders will change their collective stance when lack of control of the Internet within their countries equates to lack of control over citizens of the nations. Dictatorships and other forms of totalitarian government structure retain only fragile control over their people.

Giving them full access to the information and ideas freely discussed in democratic societies could have the effect of lessening that control, perhaps even contributing to its end.

Chapter 2

Bureaucratic Power

Bureaucracy was defined by German sociologist *Max Weber* as a form of organization characterized by hierarchical chains of command, a specialized division of labor, clearly specified authority and reporting to superiors, formal goal orientation, and impersonality in the sense of reliance on merit systems and uniform treatment of clients rather than on family or other particularistic characteristics.

By the U.S. Government Bureaucracy was defined as The structure and personnel of organizations, rooted in formal rules and informal processes, that collectively function as the core system of U.S. government and that both determine and carry out public policies using a high degree of specialized expertise.

However, the word bureaucracy often has a highly emotional, negative, prescriptive meaning. To those, bureaucracy is a simply way to complicated, and to make things more difficult than should be, as this little funny story can show:

Lord spoke to Noah and said:

-Noah, in six months I am going to make it rain until the whole is covered with water and all the evil things are destroyed. But, I want to save a few good people and two of every living on the planet. I am ordering you to build an ark.

"*Ok*", Noah said, trembling with fear and fumbling with the blueprints, "*I'm you man*".

-Six months and it start to rain, thundered the Lord.

-You better have my ark completed or learn to swim for a long, long time.

Six months passed, the sky began to cloud up, and the rain began to fall in torrents. The Lord looked down and saw Noah sitting in his yard, weeping, and there was no ark.

-Noah ! shouted the Lord

-Where is ark ?–A lightning bolt crashed into the ground right beside Noah.

"Lord, please forgive me !" begged Noah. "*I did my best, but there were some big problems. First, I had to get a building permit for the ark's construction, but your plans did not meet their code. So, I had to hire an enginer to redo the plans, only to get into a long argument with him about whether to include a fire-sprinkler system. My neighbors objected, so I had to get a variance from the city planning board.*

Then, I had a big problem getting enough wood for the ark, because there was a ban on cutting trees to save the spotted owl. I tried to convinve the environmentalists and the U.S. Fish and Wildlife Service that I need the wood to save the owls, but they wouldn't let me catch them, so no owls.

Next,I started gathering up the animals but got sued by an animal rights group that objected to me taking along only two of each kind.

Just when the suit got dismissed, the EPA notified me that I couldn't complete the ark without filing an environmental impact statement on your proposed flood. They didn't take kindly to the idea that they had no jurisdiction over the conduct of a Supreme Being.

Then, the Corps of Engineers wanted a map of the proposed flood plan. I sent them a globe !

Right now, I'm still trying to resolve a complain with the Equal Opportunities Commission overr how many minorities I'm supposed to hire.

The IRS has seized all my assets claiming that I am trying to leave the country, and I just got notice from the state that I owe some kind of use tax. Really, I don't think I can finish the ark in less than five years."

With that, the sky cleared, the sun began to shine, and a rainbow arched across the sky. Noah looked up and smiled. "You mean you are not going to destroy the world ?" he asked hopefully.

-*No*-said the Lord, and continued: *The Government already has*

The idea that the government has too much bureaucracy is what almost anyone thinks. The presidency, the Government bureaucracies are frequently pictured as "overwhelmingly large". Statistics are frequently cited to shore up this argument: data that indicate that U.S. bureaucracy is the largest employer in the country, consuming a quarter of the Gross National Product, and that it is the fourth-largest bureaucracy in the world-behind only Russia, China, and India in numbers of employees. United States public bureaucracy spends more than a trillion dollars annually. All such data are accurate—but only partly.

United States bureaucracy is not one massive organization but numerous small units, mostly very small ones situated at the grass roots. Actually there are over 80,000 U.S. bureaucracies—or, more precisely, 1 Federal government, 50 state bureaucracies, and 83,649 local public bureaucracies with 19,296 municipalities; 16,666 townships; 33,131 special districts; 3,043 counties; and 14,556 school districts. Of these, 30,913 public organizations have no full time employees. And only 1,159 have more than 1,000 employees—and nearly one-third or 493 of these are school districts, which means that the bulk of "big" bureaucracy is in reality made up of very small organizational units located at the grass roots. Many of the big public organizations on the local level are school systems

THE GROWTH OF BUREAUCRATIC POWER

There are several reasons for the growth of bureaucratic power over time:

1. *Stability.* Bureaucracies outlast elected officials and presidents, developing their own policy culture which has great inertia and is difficult to change.

2. *Implementation.* Bureaucracy is not constitutionally given power to set policy, but it does because it has to, given its role in making the necessary day-to-day rulings and decisions inherent in implementing policy at a practical level.

3. *Regulation.* Bureaucracy is routinely charged with developing the formal rules which implement legislation. The *Federal Register* publishes some 60,000 pages of such rules annually.

4. *Adjudication.* Bureaucracy also routinely has to make judicial-like decisions about individual cases. This is particularly true of regulatory agencies like the National Labor Relations Board, the Federal Communications Commission, and the Equal Employment Opportunity Commission.

5. *Administrative discretion.* Even in the most routine tasks, there is some administrative leeway in decision-making. For instance, IRS audit agents have some discretion in deciding which rules to apply to a taxpayer's form.

6. *Budgeting.* Bureaucrats believe in their programs and seek to maximize their budgets in general, and when possible, to maximize the percentage of their budget which is in *discretionary funds* that give bureaucrats more decision-making power.

The Extend of the Federal Bureaucracy

Some 2.8 million civilians work for the federal government, and another 1.4 million in the armed forces. They are organized into 14 cabinet departments, 60 independent agencies, and a large Executive Office of the President. Together with the 50 state governments and some 86,000 local governments, their collective budget of $2.5 trillion is about 34-35% of U. S. gross domestic product (GDP). Of this, the federal share is about two-thirds. By comparison, around 1900 federal spending was only about 2% of GDP and the federal government was much smaller relative to the states. Still, the governmental percentage of GDP today is about the same as in Japan and is less than in Canada or most European countries.

The Cabinet departments like the Department of Health and Human Services (HSS) employ 60% of all federal workers. They are headed by a secretary (attorney general in the case of the Justice Department) who is appointed by and reports to the president. Cabinet status gives prominence to an issue, as Woodrow Wilson did in creating the Department of Labor in 1913 or Lyndon Johnson did in creating the Department of Housing and Urban Development in 1965. Outside the departments are *independent regulatory commissions* which regulate a given area, such as the Environmental Protection Agency or the Federal Communications Commission.

A few regulatory agencies remain inside a department, like the Food and Drug Administration inside HHS. *Government corporations* like the U. S. Post Office are another form of governmental organization.

Bureaucracy and Democracy

The *spoils system* associated with the administration of Andrew Jackson epitomized the selection of government employees on the basis of party loyalty, electoral support, and political influence. The Pendleton Act of 1883 created the Civil Service Commission (now the Merit Systems Protection Board, MSPB) and established the merit system for 10% of government employees. As each new president "blanketed in" his appointments into the merit system, to protect his appointments from being replaced by a successor, the proportion covered by the civil service gradually grew to around 90%. While today the bureaucracy reflects minorities and women overall, these groups are under-represented in the higher ranks of the federal bureaucracy.

While reducing spoils and favoritism, the civil service system has created problems of *responsiveness* (getting bureaucrats to be accountable to the president) and *productivity* (creating performance-based rewards). Jimmy Carter's Civil Service Reform Act of 1978[1] replaced the Civil Service Commission with the Office of Personnel Management and the MSPB in order to separate out its merit systems and productivity functions. The act also created the Senior Executive Service (SES), an attempt to give more discretion of assignment and rewards to top administrators.

Nonetheless, rates of dismissal of bureaucrats, favoritism in giving bonuses, and other indicators seem to show little effect of the reform.

---

[1] Civil Service Reform Act of 1978: Created the Senior Executive Service.
Created the Merit Systems Protection Bd.
Created Office of Personnel Management
Abolished the Civil Service Commission

Bureaucratic Politics

The president retains direct control over appointment of some 3,000 positions, including Cabinet officers, diplomats, and federal judges. For these "plums," political loyalty is balanced against competence. Congress has tried to increase its influence with the Whistleblower Protection Act of 1989, protecting those who report policy and administrative abuses. Over time, however, every bureaucracy tends to develop its own *agency culture* which is difficult to control. Likewise, few get federal jobs solely through the formal merit system of exams. Rather, people inside an agency contact their friends and associates when a position becomes vacant and applicants are able to apply through the OPM well before formal lists of vacancies are printed. Networks develop around shifting career lines among federal, state and local, and private and non-profit organizations in the same field.

The Bureaucracy and the Budgetary Process

In January, almost two years before the start of the federal fiscal year on October 1, the Office of Management and Budget presents long-range forecasts of revenues and expenditures to the president. The president and the OMB develop guidelines for all federal agencies, which prepare and submit budget requests by July. The OMB reviews agency requests and holds budget hearings in August through September of the year before. In November and December, the OMB presents a revised budget to the president and a budget message is prepared and presented to Congress in January of the year in which the fiscal year starts.

From February through May the Congressional Budget Office reviews the budget and reports to the House and Senate budget committees. From May through June these committees establish the "first concurrent resolution," which sets the overall total for budget outlays in major categories. From July through September, appropriations committees and subcommittees draw up detailed appropriations and submit them to the congressional budget committees for the "second concurrent resolution." The full House and Senate pass the second concurrent resolution, reconciling the overall budget targets of the House and Senate. In September and October the House and Senate pass the actual appropriations bills funding the departments and agencies of government.

Since the fiscal year begins October 1, Congress often must pass "continuing resolutions" to fund government in the interim until passage of appropriations bills.

The Politics of Budgeting

Budgeting is *incremental*, accepting as legitimate the previous year's expenditures and focusing instead on requested changes. Reformers have proposed such schemes as *zero-based budgeting* and *sunset laws* to try to force Congress to consider base expenditures and whether agencies should be renewed at all, but Congress is taxed to the limit simply to consider requested changes. Decision-making is further hampered because submitted budgets are *nonprogrammatic*—that is, budget requests are usually grouped into generic categories like "personnel" and "supplies," cutting across policy programs. Seemingly, *program budgeting* would remedy this, but this is difficult to implement for a variety of reasons (bureaucratic resistance due to added paperwork or perceived loss of power, difficulty in assigning overhead expenses to specific programs, and overlap of program functions served by the same resource).

Regulatory Politics

Since the fiscal year begins Federal regulations are pervasive, from enforcing auto safety by the National Transportation Safety Board to monitoring bank accounts by the Federal Deposit Insurance Corporation to banning tobacco advertisements by the Federal Communications

Commission. The *capture theory of regulation* warns that some regulatory commissions may come to represent the industries they are supposed to regulate rather than the public interest. The Federal Communications Commission has been accused of this vis-a-vis the television industry, for instance. *Activist agencies* created by Congress are least likely to be captured, partly because their functions extend across many industries. Examples are the Equal Opportunity Employment Commission (EEOC), the Occupational Safety and Health Administration (OSHA), and the Environmental Protection Agency (EPA).

Deregulation became a popular movement during the Reagan era in the 1980s, though credit for first abolishing a major regulatory agency goes to Jimmy Carter, who ended the Civil Aeronautics Board over industry objections in 1978. The nation's first regulatory agency, the Interstate Commerce Commission, established in 1887 amid the populist movement, was stripped of most of its power in the 1980s and was abolished in 1995. Today there are counter current s, calling for *re-regulation* of the airline industry in the face of congestion and air travel delays, and for tighter control over the financial industry following the $200 billion "bail out" of savings and loans.

Congressional Constraints on the Bureaucracy

Congress has placed a number of constraints on the federal bureaucracy:

1. *The Administrative Procedures Act of 1946 (APA)* required agencies to post proposed rules in the *Federal Register*, solicit comments, and hold hearings.

2. *The Freedom of Information Act of 1966 (FOIA)* gave citizens a formal route for forcing agencies to divulge information, with some broad exceptions.

3. *The Privacy Act of 1974* required agencies to keep confidential the personal records of individuals, especially Social Security and Internal Revenue Service files.

Other congressional constraints come in the form of Senate confirmation of federal appointments, committee hearings on federal programs, congressional investigations, congressional case work for constituents, and the appropriations process itself.

Interest Groups and Bureaucratic Decision-Making

Interest groups scrutinize federal agencies even more closely than Congress, bringing good and bad points to the attention of Congress and the press. For instance, the Sierra Club is one of several groups which monitors the Environmental Protection Agency. Agencies, in turn, may owe much to interest groups which lobby Congress on their behalf at appropriations time (the EEOC owes its existence to civil rights groups, for example). Interest groups also testify at hearings, hold press conferences, undertake advertising campaigns, solicit media support, and mobilize grass-roots followers.

Judicial Constraints on the Bureaucracy

The courts routinely hear cases dealing with alleged bureaucratic overstepping of authority. They may even issue *injunctions* against agency actions before they happen. Usually, however, agencies have been successful in defending themselves in court, partly because of their superior legal resources. One study showed the court success rate of various agencies varied from 56% by the Immigration and Naturalization Service to 91% by the Federal Trade Commission.

Final

The U.S. bureaucracy stands at the very heart of the governing processes and influences the ways we live, work, and act, bureaucratic institutions are worth knowing about. Students of U.S. government devote considerable attention to the study of the legislative processes and to an examination of how the presidency influences decisions in government and how the courts use theirs interpretative functions to affect lives and livelihoods, But frequently the most critical element of bureaucracy's role within U.S. government is neglected or mentioned only in passing.

A typical U.S. Government textbook devotes only a few pages, if the, to bureaucracy's roles and influences, while the presidency, the Congress, and the Supreme Court may be given several chapters of commentary, description, and analysis. Although those institutions attract more attention from the media, a well-rounded understanding of governmental processes also necessitates a study of bureaucracy. Bureaucracy is not merely the passive, routine implementor of the laws enacted elsewhere in government It is not a machine. It is am active partner in the political processes and as such is involved in deciding "who gets what, where, when, and how". Understanding how these decisional processes work, why they work the way they do, the manner in which they affect our lives, and their possibilities for change and reform is not only intellectually satisfying, it is a basic step to becoming knowledgeable about how modern U.S. government operates.

Bureaucracy is an increasing source of employment. Knowing about possibilities for employment in this area and about the setting where many work today—the possibilities and constraints of working within U.S. public bureaucracy—will be helpful to those thinking about careers in this field.

It is to our own advantage to know how public bureaucracy works. It serve our self-interest to be as informed as we can be about this subject, which is so vital to our lives and livelihoods.

Chapter 3

Public Budgeting

Each year, the federal government raises and spends more than $1.5 trillion through its budget process. The federal budget process is widely regarded as a complex, time-consuming, and arcane set of activities often suffused with controversy, frustration, and delay. Budgeting for the federal government is not a single process; rather it consists of a number of processes that have evolved separately and which occur with varying degrees of coordination.

These characteristics of the process are attributable to various factors, including the vast scope and complexity of federal activities and the numerous types of financial transactions needed to fund them, the profusion of participants in the budget process and the wide dispersal of budgetary power, and the far-reaching economic and political consequences of budgetary decision-making.

In a sense the term "budget process" is a misnomer when applied to the federal government. This research paper attempt to clarify the role played by each of the component parts of the budget process as well as how they operate together.

The budget cycle

The federal budget cycle begins each year with the preparation and submission to Congress of the President's budget. The President's budget is only a request to Congress; Congress is not required to adopt his recommendations. Nevertheless, the President's budgetary proposals often guide congressional revenue and spending decisions, though the extent of the influence varies from year to year and depends more on political and fiscal conditions than on the legal status of the budget. The Constitution grants the "power of the purse" to Congress, but does not establish any specific procedure for consideration of budgetary legislation.

The Budget and Accounting Act of 1921, as codified in Title 31 of the *United States Code*, established the basis for an executive budget process and created the Bureau of the Budget (reorganized as the Office of Management and Budget (OMB) in 1970) to assist him in carrying out his responsibilities as well as the General Accounting Office (GAO) to assist Congress as the principle auditing agency of the federal government.

The Act requires the President to submit a *proposed budget* [1] by the first Monday in February for the next fiscal year, which begins October 1. Although this budget does not itself have the force of law, it is a comprehensive look at government revenues and spending and the start of a dialogue with Congress.

The Congressional Budget and Impoundment Control Act of 1974 (PL 93-344) established the House and Senate Budget Committees and provided for the annual adoption of a concurrent resolution on the

---

[1] The White House's OMB prepares the Budget proposal, after receiving directions from the President and consulting with his senior advisors and officials from Cabinet departments and others agencies.

budget as a mechanism for facilitating congressional budgetary decision making. This Act also established the Congressional Budget Office (CBO) to provide budgetary information to Congress independent of the executive branch.

In response to the President's budget proposal, congressional committees hold hearings and submit their views and estimates of spending and revenues within their respective jurisdictions to the House or Senate Budget Committees. With this information, the Budget Committees draft and report a concurrent resolution on the budget to their respective houses.

While it also does not have the force of law, the concurrent resolution on the budget is the central part of the budget process in Congress. It is an agreement between the House and Senate, which establishes an outline for all subsequent budgetary actions, and has a coordinating effect on the efforts of other committees. Spending and revenue laws are subsequently enacted separately. Enforcement of the budget resolution is accomplished by points of order against legislation that would violate its strictures, and through enactment of legislation in response to reconciliation instructions.

Although the budget resolution does not mention specific programs or accounts, aggregates, functional categories, and reconciliation instructions (if any) are predicated on non-binding assumptions which provide a guideline for subsequent actions. These guidelines are implemented through a process of "crosswalking" the amounts in functional categories to each committee with jurisdiction over spending under sections 302(a) and 602(a) of the Congressional Budget Act.

The budget resolution also provides a guideline for the overall level of revenues, but not for their composition. Committees with jurisdiction over revenues, entitlements, or other mandatory spending1 not directly controlled though the annual appropriations process are then responsible for reporting any necessary legislation to their respective chamber to insure that revenue and spending conform to these allocations. In some years, the budget resolution includes reconciliation instructions.

All committees receiving such instructions submit their recommendations to the Budget Committee in their chamber, which packages them as an omnibus measure and reports it without substantive revision. The reconciliation process has become the chief avenue for achieving the changes in revenues and entitlements necessary to implement the overall budget plan established in the budget resolution.

In addition, the budget resolution specifies an appropriate level of public debt to reflect the budgetary policies agreed upon in the resolution. In 1979, the House adopted a rule (House Rule XLIX) which deems the amount of public debt agreed to in the conference report on the budget resolution to be automatically agreed to as a separate joint resolution which is sent to the Senate. The Senate does not have an equivalent rule and must therefore consider the House joint resolution or some other legislation to raise the debt limit, if an increase is needed.

The annual appropriations process provides funding for discretionary programs through the consideration of 13 appropriations bills. Congress must enact these measures prior to the start of each fiscal year (October 1) or provide for the affected programs in a continuing resolution.

By custom, the House initiates all appropriations measures, although the Senate may amend them as it sees fit. The House and Senate Appropriations Committees are organized into 13 subcommittees, which are each responsible for reporting one of these measures.

These appropriations bills are constrained by the total amount allocated under the budget resolution as well as by the guidelines established separately in authorizing legislation. Authorizations may be permanent or temporary, and their provisions may be general or specific, but they do not themselves provide funding in the absence of appropriations actions.

Congressional budgetary actions are also restricted by two control mechanisms established under the Budget Enforcement Act of 1990. These restrictions entail a spending cap to limit the total amount of discretionary spending, and a pay-as-you-go process to require an offset to any congressional actions on entitlements or revenues which would increase the deficit. Under either process, congressional actions which violate these strictures would trigger a presidential order for an across the board cut of nonexempt programs (known as a sequester) in the affected area.

After submitting his budget, the President's role in the budget process is an informal one until budgetary legislation is presented for his signature. The President may either sign or veto any measure presented to him in its entirety. Beginning in 1997, once a measure becomes law, new presidential impoundment authority granted under the Line Item Veto Act of 1995 (PL 104-130) will allow the President to cancel spending for specified items.

He will be able to submit a special rescission message within 20 days of the enactment of an appropriation measure or accompanying a January budget message canceling any dollar amount of discretionary budget authority, any item of new direct spending, or any limited tax benefit. The specified budget authority in such a message will be canceled unless a subsequent disapproval bill is enacted. In addition, any funds rescinded under this authority will be for deficit reduction, and unavailable to be reallocated for other spending.

Budget Coverage and Classifications

On-Budget and Off-Budget Entities: For the past several decades, the federal budget has merged together trust funds and federal funds into a single presentation, with certain exceptions. Entities included in the budget presentation are referred to as on-budget entities; those excluded are known as off-budget entities. At present, the Social Security trust funds and the postal service fund are the only off-budget entities. Despite their off-budget status, the President's budget includes information on the budgetary impact of these funds.

Operating and Capital Funds: The federal government does not use separate operating and capital budgets, unlike most state governments. Instead, funds for operating expenses and capital programs are merged together. However, the President's annual budget submission includes an analysis of such funds in the budget.

Functional Categories: One of the most long-standing methods of classifying federal spending is by functional category. The functional categories—such as national defense, agriculture, transportation, and health—are used to group together related spending accounts regardless of the agency or other unit that manages them. The functional categories thus represent a broad statement of budget priorities.

Discretionary and Direct (Mandatory) Spending: A more recent method of classifying federal spending, arising from the procedural requirements of the Budget Enforcement Act of 1990, depends on whether the spending is considered to be discretionary or direct. Discretionary spending[2] is

---

[2] *Discretionary spending,* which accounts for one-third of all Federal spending, is what the President and Congress must decide to spend for the next year through the 13 annual appropriations bills. It includes money for such activities as the FBI and the Coast Guard, for housing and education, for space exploration and highway construction, and for defense and foreign aid.

provided in annual appropriations acts, which fall under the jurisdiction of the House and Senate Appropriations committees. Direct spending[3], also called mandatory spending, is provided in substantive legislation, which is within the jurisdiction of the authorizing committees of the House and Senate. Most direct spending involves entitlement programs funded by permanent appropriations. Some entitlement programs, however, are funded in annual appropriations acts, but such spending is considered to be direct spending.

Key Budget Concepts and Terms

A thorough understanding of the federal budget process requires familiarity with dozens, if not hundreds, of concepts and terms. Some of the key concepts and terms relating to the elementary units of budgeting, budget coverage and classifications, the timing of budgetary actions, and the budget baseline are discussed below.

Elementary Units of Budgeting

Like any complex process, federal budgeting can be broken down into its fundamental units of activity and measurement.

Spending: The spending process encompasses three distinct phases involving budget authority, obligations, and outlays. Budget authority is enacted by Congress and the President in law. It provides the legal basis

---

3 *Mandatory spending,* which accounts for two-thirds of all spending, is authorized by permanent laws, not by the 13 annual appropriations bills. It includes entitlements-such as Social Security, Medicare, Veterans' benefits, and Food Stamps-through which individuals receive benefits because they are eligible based on their age, income, or other criteria. It also includes interest on the national debt, which the Government pays to individuals and institutions that hold Treasury bonds and other Government Securities. The President and Congress can change the law in order to change the spending on entitlements and other mandatory programs-but they don't have to.

for federal agencies to make binding financial commitments in the form of obligations. Obligations stem from such agency actions such as entering into contracts, employing personnel, and submitting orders for goods and services. When obligations are liquidated, outlays ensue. Usually, outlays take the form of checks, electronic fund transfers, or other payments made by the Treasury Department.

Most of the new budget authority made available to agencies each year derives automatically from laws enacted during prior Congresses. The funds become available without the Congress taking any legislation action. For example, the funds necessary to pay Social Security benefits are provided automatically each year under a law enacted in the 1930s providing a permanent appropriation for the program.

Other forms of budget authority which may bypass annual legislative action include borrowing authority and contract authority, under which agency heads may borrow funds or enter into contractual arrangements in advance of appropriations action, and the authority to spend offsetting collections (see discussion under Revenues, below). The remaining new budget authority made available to agencies each year comes from currently enacted legislation, mostly in the form of measures providing annual appropriations. Many agencies have access to additional budget authority enacted in prior years that has carried over as unspent balances.

One of the most important characteristics of budget authority is the period during which it is available for obligation. Most budget authority for the routine operating expenses of the federal government is 'one-year' funding, meaning that it may be obligated only during the one fiscal year for which it is made available; after that, the funds lapse and no longer are available to be obligated. Budget authority enacted for procurement, construction, and similar long-term activities, on the other hand, often is 'multiyear' or 'no-year' funding, which may be obligated during a set number of fiscal years or an indefinite period. For all types of budget authority, outlays usually may be made for several fiscal years after the authority to obligate the funds has expired.

The measurement of the pace at which spending for particular programs occurs is referred to as the spendout rate. More precisely, this measures the rate at which budget authority becomes outlays during fiscal year periods. Spendout rates are determined largely by the timing of agency activity. Consequently, it is more difficult for Congress to control outlay levels than it is to control budget authority levels.

In the case of some spending programs, the federal government lends funds directly or guarantees them as a third party. For many years, the federal budget monitored such credit activities by tracking the level of direct loan obligations and loan guarantee commitments. Pursuant to the Federal Credit Reform Act of 1990 (incorporated into the Congressional Budget Act of 1974 as a new Title V by the Budget Enforcement Act of 1990), the federal budget now focuses on the subsidy element, rather than the cash flows, of these two types of programs. Loan subsidies now are recorded as budget authority and outlays.

Revenues: Revenues of the federal government (also referred to as receipts) derive from a number of sources. Individual and corporate income taxes account for about half of the receipts of the federal government, but social insurance taxes are an increasingly prominent source of revenues. Additional amounts accrue to the government from various excise taxes, customs fees, gifts, and miscellaneous receipts.

Some income to the federal government, which arises from business-like or market-oriented activities (such as the sale of electricity from federal power administrations), is referred to as offsetting collections. These funds are offset or deducted from federal spending instead of being counted as revenues.

Deviations from the 'normal' tax code (such as exemptions, deductions, and special rules) are known as tax expenditures. These devices provide a means of pursuing policy objectives in a manner analogous to spending programs. For example, the federal government promotes the goal of homeownership by providing a tax deduction for mortgage interest costs; comparable resources could be devoted to this goal through spending programs involving grants or loans.

Accounts and Funds: Spending and revenues in the federal budget are recorded on the basis of accounts. In the case of annual appropriations, for example, each account usually corresponds to a separate heading in the legislation. Funds allocated to accounts are further divided by the programs, projects, activities, and objects of expenditure related to the account. In budget presentations, accounts are usually grouped together by the organizational unit (e.g. the department or agency) that manages them. Some types of accounts, such as credit financing accounts, are included in budget presentations but are used only for accounting purposes; they do not reflect budgetary transactions.

Federal spending and revenues also may be characterized by the type of funds involved. The two basic types of funds in the budget are trust funds, which are used to carry out specific purposes in accordance with statutory requirements, and federal funds, which derive from the federal government's sovereign powers and are spent on the government's general activities.

Deficit and Surplus: The deficit or surplus is determined by the relationship of outlays to revenues. An excess of outlays over revenues is a deficit, while an excess of revenues over outlays is a surplus.

A history of Deficits and Surpluses

The government incurred its first deficit in 1792, and it generated 70 annual deficits between 1900 and 1997. For most of the Nation's history, deficits were the results of either wars or recessions. Wars necessitated major increases in military spending, while recessions reduced Federal tax revenues from businesses and individuals.

The government generated deficits during the War of 1812, the recession of 1837, the Civil War, the depression of the 1890s, and World War I. Once the war ended or the economy began to grow, the Government followed its deficits with budget surpluses, with which it paid down the debt.

Deficits returned in 1931 and remained for the rest of the decade—due to the Great Depression and the spending associated with President Roosevelt's new Deal. Then, World War II forced the nation to spend unprecedented amounts on defense and to incur corresponding unprecedented deficits. Since then—with Democratic and Republican Presidents, Democratic and Republican Congresses—the Government has balanced its books only ten times, most recently last year.

Nevertheless, the deficits before 1981 paled in comparison to what followed. That year, the Government cut income tax rates and greatly increased defense spending, but it did early 1980s reduced Federal revenues, increased Federal outlays for unemployment insurance and similar progrmas that are closely tied to economic conditions and forced the Government to pay interest on moree national debt at a time when interest rates were high.as a result, the deficit soared.

The United States have been able to move from deficit to balance, because spending growth has been restrained. Outlays are growing slower than revenues. Revenues have stayed relatively constant, at around 16 to 20 percent of GDP, since the 1960s. In that time, however, outlays grew from about 17 percent of GDP in 1965 to nearly 24 percent in 1983 before failing below 119 percent today.

Since 1983, spending has been reduced or held constant as a percent of GDP across a wide variety of programs. The most significant reduction has occurred in discretionary spending, which has fallen from 10.3 percent to 6.3 percent in 1999. Combined spending on social security and net interest has remained roughly constant at about 7 ½ percent of GDP from 1983 to 1997. However, the debt reduction of the last two years has brought this spending down to 6.7 percent of GDP in1999. A similar path has been followed in the rest of mandatory spending in total, but only because the grown in Medicare and Medicaid has been offset by declines in other mandatory spending.

Put simply, a surplus occurs when revenues exceed spending in any year—just as a deficit occurs when spending exceeds revenues. Generally, to finance past deficits, the Treasury has borrowed money. With certain exceptions, the debt is the sum total of U.S. deficits, minus our surpluses, over the years.

Clinton's Administration

In 1993, President Clinton and the Congress made another effort to cut the deficit. They enacted a five-year deficit reduction package of spending cuts and higher revenues. The laws was designed to cut the accumulated deficits from1994 to1998 by about $ 500 billion. The new law extend the limits on discretionary spending and the "pay-as-you-go" rules.

Although the 1993 plan exceeded all expectations in reducing the deficit, the task of reaching balance would require one final push. That would come with the historic 1997 Balanced Budget Act (BBA).

Originally designed to balance the budget by 2002, the BBA provided for $ 247 billion in savings over five years. It also extended the solvency of Medicare's trust fund for at least 10 years while providing for the largest investment in higher education since the G.I. Bill in 1945, the largest investment in children's health care since the creation of Medicaid in 1965, and a % 500-per-child tax credit about 27 million working families.

Clearly, the President's deficit reduction efforts have paid off. In 1998, the Federal budget reported its first surplus ($69 billion) since 1969. In 1999, the surplus nearly doubled to $ 124 billion. As a result of these surpluses, Federal debt held by the public has been reduced from $ 3.8 trillion at the end of 1997 to $ 3.6 trillion at the end of 1999. With continued prudent fiscal policies, the budget can remain in surplus for many years. Under the President Clinton Budget proposals, the Federal debt held by the public would be fully paid back by 2013.

Final

But, should the American people be worry about the possibility of a return to budget deficits? The 2001 Budget forecast surplus for decades to come, if the government maintain the policy of fiscal discipline and strategic investments.

Budget deficits force the Government to borrow money in the private capital markets. That borrowing competes with borrowing by business that want to build factories and machiness that make workers more productive and raise incomes, and borrowing by families who hope to buy new homes, cars, and other goods. The competition for funds tends to produce higher interest rates.

Deficits increase the Federal debt and, with it, the Government obligation to pay interest. The more it must pay in interest, the less it has available to spend on education, law enforcement, and other important services, or the more it must collect in taxes—forever after. As recently as 1997, the Government spent over 15 percent of its budget to pay interest, in contrast to a projected 11 percent for 2001. Continuing surplus will reduce these interest payments futher in future years.

In the end, the surplus is a decision about the future of the American people. Our hope is that the Government provide a solid foundation for future generations, just as parents try to do within a family. For a Nation, this means a strong economy and low interest rates and debt.

Chapter 4

Regulations
A Economic Impact

The government acts in many ways. The most familiar role of the government is the subject of public finance courses. The government raises resources in taxes and then spends this money through various expenditure efforts. In addition, the governement also regulates the behavior of firms and individuals. Our legal systems is perhaps the most comprehensive example of the mechanism by which this regulation takes place.

The firms behavior regulations involves much more than attempting to deal with monopoly power in the traditional text book sense. The setting of prices for public utilities, the control of pollution emitted in the firm's production process, and the allocation of radio broadcast bands are all among the contexts in which government regulation lays a prominent role in influencing firm behavior.

The behavior of individuals has also come under increasing regulatory scrutiny. In some cases, decisions are regulated directly, such as the requirement to wear seatbelts. In addition, individuals are affected by regulations that influence either market prices or the mix of products that are available. Product-safety standards, for example, serve to eliminate the high-risk end of the product-quality spectrum.

The menu of products available to consumers and jobs available to workers is the subject of substancial regulatory influence.

To assess the pervasiveness of these efforts, consider a day in the life of the typical American worker. That worker awakes in the morning to the sound of his clock radio, where the stations he listens to and the wavelength they broadcast on are regulated by the Federal Communications Commission. And the Food and Drug Administration to avoid misleading consumers about the health benefits of breakfast cereals. The orange juice from concentrate can also no longer be labeled "fresh" courtesy of a 1991 Federal Trade Commission Action. The milk poured on the cereal is also regulated in a variety of ways; perhaps the most important being the role of U.S. Department of Agriculture price supports (milk marketing orders). More recently, there has been the object of substantial regulatory debate. If one choses to add fruit to cereal, it is reassuring to know that the Environmental Protection Agency (EPA) stringently regulates the pesticides that can be used on domestic produce.

Heading to work, our regulated individual climbs into a japanese car that was successful in not violating any import quotas. The worker will be safer en route to work than in earlier years, thanks to extensive safety regulations by the National Highway Traffic Safety Administration. The fuel used by the car is also less environmentally damaging than would have been the case in the absence of U.S. Department of Transportation Fuel Economy standards and in the absence of EPA gasoline lead standards

Once on the job, the worker is protected against many of the hazards of work by occupational safety and health regulations and is also assured a decent wage by minimum-wage regulation. A host of U.S. Department of Labor Regulations, as well as Equal Employement Opportunity Commission stipulations, ensure that the worker will not be unduly discriminated against during the course of this employment.

Our worker's phone calls are billed at telephone rates set by regulation, although increasingly these rates have been influenced by market forces. Visiting business associates travel on planes whose availability and fares have been greatly influenced by regulatory changes. The safe arrival of these associates is due in part to the continued vigilance of the Federal Aviation Administration and the safety incentives created by tort liability lawsuits following airplane crashes.

Even when our individual escapes from work for an evening of relaxation and recreation, government regulations remain present. If the worker eats dinner at a restaurant, there is a good chance that he or she will be forbidden to smoke cigarettes or relegated to a smoking area. The U.S. Consumer Product Safety Commission, for example, has regulatory responsibility for a wide range of sports equipment, ranging from all-terrain vehicles to baseball helmets.

Although some deregulation has taken place in the past decade, the scope of government regulation remains quite broad. The role of regulation in our society remains ubiquitous. Various forms of government regulation touch almost every aspect of our activities and consumption patterns. The widespread impact of regulation is not unexpected, in as much as this represents a very potent mechanism by which the government can influence market outcomes. Before we go deeper in the discussion of regulation and deregulation, let us review the history of regulation.5

The government has not always interfered with corporations, however, the first cases of regulation occurred around the late 1870s, with regard to the railroad industry.

Throughout the Nineteenth Century, the railroad industry developed at a furious pace. As corporations began to form, the danger of monopolies quickly became apparent. A group of organized farmers, known as the Grangers, lobbied for regulation of the industry, to save themselves from the unfair prices and practices of the railroad companies. In 1877, the Supreme Court case of Munn v. Illinois questioned the validity of an Illinois law fixing maximum rates for storage of grain. The Chicago warehouse of Munn and Scott protested, believing that they were being denied property without due process of law. The court ruled that the warehouse business was sufficiently "clothed with public interest" to justify public control. The consequence of this case was the setting of a precedent that states have the right to regulate interstate commerce. Furthermore, the court said that "until Congress makes use of its power, a state might act even if in so doing it may indirectly operate upon commerce outside its jurisdiction."

For a few years, the states controlled the railroad industry. However, the laws that were developed to protect the states' right to control businesses were largely ineffectual. The inability of a state government to hold companies to its regulations made the need for federal legislation painfully apparent. In the Supreme Court case of Wabash, St. Louis, and Pacific Railway Company v. Illinois, it was ruled that "no state can exercise any control over commerce which passes beyond its limits." This ruling completely reversed previously enacted legislation. To this day, regulation of interstate commerce falls in the hands of the federal government.

Federal regulation of businesses officially began in 1887, with the passing of the Interstate Commerce Act. This created the first independent regulatory commission. It was originally "devised to apply technical expertise and a semijudicial and less partisan approach to the regulation of complex affairs." At first, it was a five person committee; all members were nominated by the president. Today, it has eleven members with a chairperson. The Interstate Commerce Commission's first act was to ensure "just and reasonable" rates from businesses and to prevent the formation of monopolies. Since its inception, the responsibilities of the commission have broadened to many fields, such as worker safety and anti-discrimination (Elkins Act of 1903 and Mann-Elkins Act of 1920).

On July 2, 1890, the first federal law directed against industrial combination and monopoly was enacted. Known as the Sherman Anti-Trust Act, it began to reverse the trend toward unchecked consolidation that began after the panic of 1873. This legislation stated that "every contract, combination in the form of trust or otherwise, or conspiracy, in restraint of trade or commerce among the several states, or with foreign nations, is hereby declared illegal." Though the issues of what is considered combination or a trust or what should be done with intrastate monopolies were still uncertain, this act set a strong precedent for future legislation. During the presidency of Theodore Roosevelt, the act was strengthened, revised, and put to thorough use.

Throughout the end of the 19th century and the beginning of the next, legislation regarding federal regulation was debated. Some of the most important acts were adopted during the presidency of Woodrow Wilson, who called for "regulated competition," not "regulated monopoly." Furthermore, he demanded a "body of laws which will look after the men who are sweating blood to get their foothold in the world of endeavor." In 1914, the Clayton Anti-Trust Act was passed to prohibit discrimination in prices among purchasers, exclusive deals tying a purchaser to a single supplier, and any action that "substantially lessens competition or tends to create a monopoly." At this time, the Federal Trade Commission was created to "prevent the unlawful suppression of competition."

Since it was created, the Federal Trade Commission has been altered several times. In one instance, the Robinson Patman Act of 1936 gave the commission the power to control prices of interstate commerce. In another case, the Celler-Kefauver Act of 1950 was enacted to prevent corporate merges that stifle competition and promote monopolies. These acts, though similar in nature to the original form of the FTC, served to strengthen it. In addition to the trade commission, throughout the decades, dozens of other laws have been enacted to regulate business. The Meat Inspection Act of 1906, the Securities and Exchange Act of 1934, the Truth In Packaging Act of 1966, and the Consumer Credit Protection Act of 1969, all serve to protect individuals from unfair practices perpetrated by business greed. Overwhelmingly, the precedent for controlling any business which stifles competition or acts unfairly toward individuals has been set.

From 1970 to nowdays, the number of federal regulations has grown; so too has the number of regulators enforcing them. Under Reagan administration, there were several pivotal changes in the regulatory oversight mechanism. First, President Reagan moved the oversight function from the Council on Wage and price Stability to OMB. Because OMB is responsible for setting the budgets of all regulatory agencies and has substantial authority over them, this change increases the institutional clout of the oversight mechanism. The second major shift was to increase the stringency of the tests being imposed. Instead of simply imposing a cost-effectiveness requirement, Reagan moved to a full-blown benefit-cost test in his Executive Order number 12291.[2] If, however, the benefit-cost test conflicts with the agency's legislative mandate-as it does for all risk and environmental regulations-the test is not binding.

The bird major change in the Executive Branch oversight process was the development of a formal regulatory planning process whereby the regulatory agencies would have to clear a regulatory agenda with the Office of Management and Budget. This procedure, which was accomplished through Executive Order Number 12498, which required the agency to list its forthcoming regulatory initiatives. This exercise has served to alert administration officals and the public at large as to the future of regulatory policy, on a pratical basis it has not had as much impact on policy outcomes as has the format review process, coupled with a benefit-cost test.

Although President Ronald Reagan succeeded in reversing the growing federal regulatory burden for a time, regulatory growth accelerated under President George Bush and, by all accounts, has exploded under President

---

[2] Sec.2. General Requirements. In promulgating new regulations, reviewing existing regulations, and developing legislative proposals concerning regulation, all agencies, to the extent permitted by law, shall adhere to the following requirements:

a. Administrative decisions shall be based on adequate information concerning the need for and consequences of proposed government action;

b. Regulatory action shall not be undertaken unless the potential benefits to society for the regulation outweigh the potential costs to society.

c. Regulatory objectives shall be chosen to maximize the benefits to society.

d. Among alternative approaches to any given regulatory objective, the alternative involving the least net costs to society shall be chosen; and

e. Agencies shall set regulatory priorities with the aim of maximizing the aggregate net benefitis to society, taking into account the condition of the particular industries affected by regulations, the condition of the national economy, and other regulatory actions contemplated for the future.

Bill Clinton. Initially, the Republican-led 104th Congress made reducing spending by federal regulatory agencies a priority, and this focus successfully slowed the rate of growth in new regulations. Unfortunately, those efforts were short-lived. Today, the size, scope, and cost of the federal regulatory system are increasing at record rates.

Many regulations today are either unnecessary or poorly designed and needlessly inefficient and expensive. Federal regulatory agencies have not developed a system for making rational, well-informed decisions on how to allocate limited resources efficiently to maximize health, safety, and environmental protection. The objective of reform is to help government shift its resources away from ineffective regulation to more efficient ones and business to devote its resources to becoming more innovative and productive.

The Cost of Federal Regulation

Estimating the precise costs of federal regulation is difficult. Unlike federal spending, regulatory costs are not accounted for in the budget process; and while agencies are supposed to calculate the costs and benefits of regulations, their calculations vary in quality and often grossly underestimate the true cost or substantially overestimate the benefits of regulation.

The total cost of government has been estimated at $3.38 trillion, nearly $1 trillion of which results from federal and state regulation, according to Americans for Tax Reform and the federal government is responsible for imposing more than $2,800 in regulatory costs for every man, woman, and child in America.

Of the 366 days in 1998, the average American worked 184.6 days for the government. This means that more than one-half of every dollar earned went to the government, either directly or indirectly and each American spends more than 40 workdays just to pay the cost of federal regulations. Rochester Institute of Technology Professor Thomas Hopkins estimated the total cost of federal regulation in 1998 is $700 billion. In the 1980s, these costs decreased, but they began to increase rapidly in 1991. They represent direct compliance costs, not indirect costs such as the cost of lost productivity.

According to the OMB, the total direct cost of regulation is about $300 billion, and the benefits of federal regulation total about $300 billion as well. Unlike the Hopkins estimates, these estimates exclude paperwork costs and economic transfer costs, a subject of some controversy.

Between April 1, 1997, and December 31, 1998, federal agencies issued more than 100 "major" final rules that will have an annual effect on the economy of at least $100 million. At a minimum, these regulations imposed a new $10 billion regulatory tax hike in just over 18 months. The Administration admitted that its regulatory elimination effort during this same period would do little to reduce the regulatory burden. However, the new regulatory taxes are likely to be far greater than $10 billion.

For example, just one final rule—the Environmental Protection Agency's (EPA) July 1997 final clean air regulations imposing tighter standards on particulate matter and ozone—is estimated to cost in the range of $60 billion to $100 billion annually.

To put Hopkins' estimates in perspective, current regulatory costs are about 43 percent of the size of the federal budget, which stands at more than $1.65 trillion in FY 1999, and represent about 9 percent of America's gross domestic product.

The Economic Impact and how that cost affect us

How the federal government regulates is important because it has a significant impact on the economy. A study by Richard Vedder, John M.

Olin Visiting Professor of Labor Economics and Public Policy at .the Center for the Study of American Business at Washington University in St. Louis, shows that, in addition to the costs of complying with regulations, the long-term costs of reduced productivity are high. Federal regulations cause $1.3 trillion in economic output to be lost each year. This is roughly equivalent to the entire economic output of the Mid-Atlantic region (Delaware, the District of Columbia, Maryland, New Jersey, New York, and Pennsylvania).

According to Vedder, when a business devotes resources to adhering to regulatory mandates, it is using those resources less efficiently; it is forced to operate in a less productive, more costly manner. This drag on productivity denies workers a higher standard of living.

A 1995 study by the Employment Policy Foundation, found that 19 percent of productivity slowdown in the 1970s was directly attributable to regulations imposed by the Occupational Safety and Health Administration (OSHA), and that nearly half of the slowdown in long-term productivity can be explained by rising government regulatory activity.

Although the amount of money the federal government spends each year to administer its regulatory programs is significant, it is much less than the costs imposed on businesses, private citizens, and state and local governments.

The National Association of Home Builders estimated that the regulatory costs of building a house in three metropolitan areas of the United States—Cincinnati, Ohio; Pittsburgh, Pennsylvania; and Santa Fe, New Mexico—tripled between 1974 and 1994. The significant drivers of these cost increases were environmentally related regulations, such as sewer and water fees, storm water runoff controls, and soil sedimentation and erosion controls. Increasingly, regulations affect the costs of paperwork, permits, equipment, worker training, attorneys fees, and record keeping, as well as the costs of goods and services, and innovation and economic growth. Although the direct costs of regulation typically are imposed on businesses and governments, ultimately they are passed on to American consumers in the form of higher prices, reduced quality or availability of products and services, or higher taxes.

Regulation increases the cost of employing workers and acts as a tax on job creation and employment. Mandated requirements, such as family and medical leave, while instinctively appealing, actually affect an employer's decisions about whether and when to hire an additional worker, which worker to hire, how much to pay the worker, and how long to keep that worker Employers carry the costs of federal labor laws that constrain their freedom to hire and fire workers and to engage in negotiations with employees and labor unions. For example: -

-Employers often are required to provide such benefits as health insurance, unemployment insurance, workers compensation, retirement benefits, paid family leave, or child care—the costs of which are passed on to consumers through higher prices or to workers through slowdowns in the creation of new jobs or offsetting reductions in wages.

-The rise in non-wage labor costs is one of the most important forces leading employees to lay off workers as well as utilize part-time, temporary, and contract labor.

-A 1990 study estimated that environmental regulations alone caused national employment to be 1.2 percent lower in 1990 than it otherwise would have been.

For all businesses, there is a bewildering array of size cutoffs for regulations, and these cutoffs exempt some of them from certain regulatory requirements. Not surprisingly, employers have strong incentives to keep their workforce just below these cutoffs. For example:

-Companies with 14 or fewer employees are exempt from the Americans with Disabilities Act.

-Employers with 19 or fewer workers are exempt from the Age Discrimination Act.

-A cluster of regulations take effect when a company hires its 50th employee.

-Affirmative action programs apply to companies working on government contracts, as do the Family and Medical Leave Act and other laws.

The American economy would enjoy substantial and long-lasting benefits from regulatory reform. There is an ever-growing body of evidence that suggests that such reform would increase productivity, lower prices, eliminate shortages, and stimulate innovation and consumer choice, ultimately enhancing economic growth.

The Benefits of Deregulation

In a recently released study entitled Economic Deregulation and Customer Choice: Lessons for the Electric Industry, Robert Crandall of the Brookings Institution in Washington, D.C., and Jerry Ellig of the Center for Market Processes at George Mason University in Fairfax, Virginia, documented the historical benefits of deregulation. Analyzing five major "network" industries that were deregulated and that share attributes with the electricity sector—natural gas, telecommunications, airlines, trucking, and railroads—Crandall and Ellig reveal that regulatory reform and customer choice generated very beneficial results. Specifically, after deregulation:

Prices fall. "Within the first two years of deregulation, prices had fallen by 4 to15 percent, and sometimes more for certain groups of customers. Within 10 years, prices were at least 25 percent lower, and sometimes close to 50 percent lower."

Service quality improves. "Deregulation and customer choice align service quality with customer desires. Crucial social goals like airline safety, reliability of gas service, and reliability of the telecommunications network were maintained or improved by deregulation and customer choice."

The rising tide lifts all boats. "Regulatory reform is not a zero sum game; it has generated genuine gains for consumers and society as a whole. It is possible to find narrowly defined groups of customers in special circumstances who paid somewhat higher prices after deregulation, but the gains to the vast majority of consumers far outweighed the effects on these small groups."

More freedom equals more benefits. "Rates fell faster in parts of the market where regulators permitted greater customer choice. Choice for all customers for all competitive services will provide the most benefits."

Final

The Crandall-Ellig study is the first to prove conclusively that the benefits of deregulation are not limited in scope to one industry. More important, it wisely rejects the notion that these findings cannot be applied to the electricity sector, which is sometimes referred to as America's last regulated monopoly. As Crandall and Ellig summarize, "Given the history of natural gas, telecommunications, airline, railroad, and trucking regulation, is it reasonable to expect that customer choice in electricity could generate consumer benefits? The experience of all these industries suggests that the answer is a resounding 'Yes'.

Chapter 5

Sexual Harassment in the Workplace and What to Do

It seems that one cannot turn the television on without hearing about someone having been sexually harassed. From the simple individual who complains about a sexual joke being told, to people who are seriously threatened by active sexual harassment that involves issues of coercion and control. There are many levels to sexual harassment and each one presents its own problems and situations. The different levels of sexual harassment are discussed as well as the reality of oppression as a result of sexual harassment.

Sexual Harassment and the legal system

Prior to the late 1970s, the concept of sexual harassment had not been described. Many women were afraid to disclose sexual harassment incidents at work for fear of being blamed for provoking them. Because this fear has not been eradicated. However, there are women who have the ability to take advantage of the power they possess in these regards. And in relationship to the law and how it protects women.

In fact, under the current legal regime, the fact that a woman aggressively pursued her boss, would not have necessarily kept her from filing a harassment suit-and possibly wangling a handsome settlement-had she later changed her mind.

That clearly demonstrate how women may well know they have the power in many cases. In this regard it would be difficult to claim that women are being oppressed these days, due to sexual harassment.

Unfortunately many women have taken advantage of the legal system when dealing with simple cases of sexual harassment that they could easily have dealt with themselves, if not ignored all together. There are many issues in the workplace that are dealt with all the time, without the interference of the administration or the law. Many people assume that just because a man may say a woman is beautiful or call her "honey" he disrespects her.

On the other hand, it may well be stated that women's oppression has been greatly lessened through the attention this subject has received through the media and through the legal profession. Women no longer need to fear being fired for no reason other than they did not want to have a sexual relationship with the boss. And likewise, a man has many more freedoms in illustrating any sexual harassment he has endured. It is quite possible that the only people who are being truly oppressed in the modern day address of sexual harassment, aside form the real wrong doers, are the individuals who must now control their personalities. They cannot tell jokes and essentially be themselves for fear of being misunderstood. Men who genuinely appreciate women for various reasons, can no longer demonstrate this in the old manner, due to the fact they can be accused of SH.

Free Speech or negative address

Sexual harassment, though able to apply to both sexes, is predominantly a concern for women in our society. Sexual harassment is a type of negative address aimed at one particular sex. It can involve something as simple as a man telling a woman a sexual joke or something as serious as forced sexual contact, There appears to be no real fine line that details where bad taste ends and sexual harassment begins, but for the most part, many women are putting men on the edge of their seats due to the power they have obtained in regards to sexual harassment.

Fortunately for the victims, times have changed and they are protected more in the workplace, but we must also understand that we live in a free speech society and should be able to voice our opinions. There is obviously a fine line between what is acceptable and what is not. And this line appears to chan and harasser attributions.

Studying the problem

There are still many activists who believe we have only scratched the surface of the problem. Such is seen in the following excerpt from an inter-sessional working group that was convened by the Commission on the Status of Women: "Whether they live in the northern hemisphere or the southern hemisphere, in a rich country or a poor one, women are subjected to violence that results in the deprivation of their fundamental human rights, this violence, which occurs in many contexts, including the home, takes various forms: physical battery, sexual and psychological abuse, harassment at the workplace and elsewhere, female foeticide, infanticide and infant neglect.

In another study, the researchers got responses from 50 male and 61 female undergraduate students at the University of Minnesota were analyzed to determine the role of gender subtypes on harasser attributions.

The findings indicated that perceived susceptibility and femininity of the victim may be important to how the gender harassment and sexual advances are perceived. Thus, the probability of viewing women as being victims of certain sexual harassment types is higher for those with less firmer perceived dispositions.

The Equal Employment Opportunity Commission (EEOC) established guidelines for the problem of sexual harassment in 1980. Since that time research on the matter of sexual harassment has increased steadily. In order to understand SH more fully, various surveys have been used in the research.

Understanding Sexual harassment

It is evidenced that one person's perception of SH is unlike another's perception. A person's perception of sexual harassment depends on several factors to include the gender of the person rating the incident, the position of the persons involved in the proposed sexual harassment incident.

For example, in an extreme case, a woman who is well known for disliking men in general, may be predisposed to believing all men are essentially sexual pigs. She may seek out every opportunity to read sexual harassment into every conversation and every action of her male co-workers. This is because she believes these attributes to be true. On the other hand, however, you can have a woman who likes men and tells jokes and calls men by names such as "baby." She may likely not be condescending to them at all, but rather merely enjoying their company. She is predisposed to accepting men. But it can also be assumed that if such a woman was approached with some sort of serious sexual harassment issue she would either deal with it herself, or take it the In between these types of situations, there are a thousand other possibilities that may occur regarding sexual harassment. This is one of the reasons why it is such a difficult issue to resolve. Each and every individual sees the same situation in a different way. One man telling a woman that she looks beautiful may incite anger, appreciation, confusion, disdain, disgust, or a myriad of other reactions. There is really no telling what simple addresses or statements will be seen as sexual harassment by which people, and in light of this it becomes very difficult for one to accurately stated whether women have been oppressed by sexual harassment cases today.

Social Interaction

Many of the researchers seen the SH as a social interaction that have to be treated, rather than as individual immoral behavior and it is important to actually discover how people defines it in the workplace.

A better understanding may be made of the so-called phenomen of sexual harassment by determining the rules that people go by, and what is inferred in behavior causality. Little is know concerning the view that people consider as what is typical when examining incidents of sexual harassment.

Many have been given lists of behavior that is potentially sexual harassment in order to ascertain their viewpoint on the matter. Based on a poll done nationally, researchers were able to develop an instrument that reflects the three types of Sexual Harassment: **UNWELCOME TOUCHING, BRIBERY AND SEXUAL ASSAULT.**

Sexual Harassment in the workplace

Sexual harassment has been a prevalent occurrence in workplaces across the country. Recent studies suggest that 40% of women and 15% of men experience some form of sexual harassment in the workplace.

Although it is illegal, it continues to happen in this politically correct era. Sexual harassment has many definitions and therefore some people find it difficult to define.

From the Legal aspect the definition has evolved and expanded considerably over the last twenty years from a narrow definitions of "quid pro quo" harassment or sexual sexual favors for economic or career rewards, to a much more expansive and sensitive definitions that includes the environment as a source of harassment, such as speech, symbols, pictures, touching, a new legal standard (the reasonable woman), and an increasing notion of punitive damages.

A particular problem for managers has been one of educating themselves and their employees about the subject and keeping abreast of new rulings. Along-accepted patterns of interaction between men and women have come into question and need to be identified and altered. Uncertainly abounds as to what constitutes sexual harassment and the seriousness of the harm inflicted by various kinds of sexual harassment in the workplace.

Finding ways to identify, monitor, and prevent sexual harassment through appropriate procedures training, as well as through formal and informal procedures mechanisms, has become an important item on the agenda of any personnel manager. Not only for the morale and effectiveness of employees but also because of legal liability.

This subject is so complex that even in the court system there have been disagreements concerning the excludability of workplace losses from their general liability policies. Liability insurance has typically been limited to providing coverage for such items as bodily harm or damage to property.

In sexual harassment cases, some courts have judged continuing employment as a property right. Others have taken a more conservative stance in the matter. If the sexual harassment is intentional, this act can be a hurdle that the insured must overcome.

Social-sexual behavior in the workplace

Social-sexual behavior in the workplace can take many forms and different labels. One topology distinguishes between non-harassing sexual behavior, direct sexual harassment, and sexualization of the workplace. Non-harassing sexual behavior includes behaviors intended as complimentary although perhaps mildly annoying for the recipient (e.g., wolf-whistling, complimentary sexual comments, and relational advances). These same behaviors may be labeled sexual harassment when they are perceived as offensive and interfere with an individual's employment. Direct sexual harassment is interpersonal, directed at a particular recipient, and may involve physical contact, coercion and force (e.g., unwelcome touching, bribery, sexual assault).

Sexualization of the workplace refers to generally indirect, non-personal sexual behaviors which create an intimidating While the realities involving simple jokes and words are obviously very simple illustrations involving sexual harassment, one the problems is that many people take these types of occurrences just as serious as the more involved aspects of sexual abuse. Many believe that it is these simple illustrations that are to blame for the more serious sexual harassment issues, due to the fact that most people let them slide. But, at the same time, men and women are nervous beyond belief, in many offices due to the threat of being pegged as a sexual harasser. A man will not be as friendly, nor will the women, when they know they must be careful of everything they say and do. Anything could be misconstrued by someone and seen as a sexual harassment issue.

According to many sources the sexual harassment complaints by men have tripled since 1991 and now make up 11.6% of cases reported to the Equal Employment Opportunity Commission, and many of these claims involve alleged same-gender sexual harassment.

Sipkins and Schmitt in his article at the National Law Journal posit that policies protecting against same-sex harassment claims that are sexual in nature should be instituted due to the ruling of the Supreme Court in the case of Oncale v. Sundowner Offshore Services, Inc.

And as stated by Roberta Graziano in her book, Sexual Harassment in the Workplace and Academia (1997), the Civil Rights Act of 1964 named sexual discrimination and granted a right for the remediation of its victims (381). Woman have had centuries of legally and culturally sanctioned abuses, therefore, this act was a fortification for womankind. Unfortunately, however, there has been little effective action by women concerning harassment in the workplace. There has actually been little progress in the area of sexual harassment and the maltreatment of women in the workplace and in schools. said, "As is often the case, laws have not always changed attitudes of employers, professors, physicians, lawyers, judges, or colleagues, and the process of redressing wrongs is frequently at least as stressful and injurious to women's mental and physical health as was the original violation of their rights. Furthermore, the harmful effects of the harassment or legal procedures on the recipient's self-esteem, self-image, career, productivity, economic well-being, and relationships are long lasting and sometimes permanent".

Sexual Harassment definition

Sexual harassment's definition is a power issue. In case after case whether the woman is a physician or one that works in a factory, sexual harassment is shown to have a similar experience to rape, abuse that is sexual, and violence that is domestic, in that the women are not believed and they, as victims, are considered at fault. A sexual harassment trial puts the woman on the defensive. She becomes drained emotionally because the lack of support for her cause.

The issue of sexual harassment is a complex one. It requires a deep understanding. Sexual harassment has clear ramifications, which have been seen to explode in scholarly as well as popular media. A a great deal has been published concerning the topic of sexual harassment, yet some questions remain unanswered. There has been no sign of sexual harassment decreasing. The 1990s have seen a barrage of instances of sexual harassment in the workplace even though most people are aware of the problem.

The court system has become somewhat responsive to the issue of sexual harassment. It is suggested that there are many instances of sexual harassment that do not reach visibility, or conclusion in the matter. Such critical dimensions as race, class, and sexual orientation are not substantially taken into account.

Even though there are laws against sexual harassment in the workplace, it perseveres as an issue that is morally degrading, hard to fight, and emotionally draining for the woman involved. Several studies have been done on the issue and one constant remains clear: each person has his or her own opinion of what constitutes sexual harassment.

What to do

Victims of Sexual harassment tend to be young, inexperienced and powerless. Specially for those the immediately and easy solution will e a informal procedures that many institutions have adopted and particularly receptive to this remedy, but the idea is also promoted as an alternative by those who run sexual harassment workshops for business and governmental agencies.

Informal procedures are based on the following assumptions:

1. That the harassment is not intentional and can be rectified by having it called to the attention of the harasser.
2. That the harasser will be responsive to verbal reprimands by superiors or counseling options identified by the informal procedures.

The focus here is on what will happen in the future rather than what happened in the past. The victim in this case will set the terms of the process by identifying what will bring her process in the hands of a hearing or grievance board.

The remedies used in this process are voluntary, not mandatory, forgiving, not punitive, unifying, not divisive. Of course, that there are cases that the only solution is when the grievance procedures is in effect, which includes:

1. Report to the supervisor or manager
2. Conduct an investigation
3. A "right to sue" letter to the victim

Employers, managers, and supervisors all have an obligation to stay within the confines of the law and to see that their employees do as well.

This means that if a supervisor sexually harasses a subordinate, the employer may be held responsible for the behavior of the supervisor, even if the employer has forbidden sexual harassment and has no knowledge of its occurrence.

Educational activities, including workshops and training sessions, can help to alter established patterns of male behavior that become offensive when women enter a male-dominated work environment.

There is some actions that all managers and supervisors should take on day-by-day basis in order to prevent sexual harassment, that includes: Providing leadership, setting the tone, making clear what behaviors will not be tolerated, taking sexual harassment complaints seriously and acting upon them promptly.

Chapter 6

Understanding Economics United States Public Finance

Public Finance, field of economics concerned with how governments raise money, how that money is spent, and the effects of these activities on the economy and on society. Public finance studies how governments at all levels—national, state, and local—provide the public with desired services and how they secure the financial resources to pay for these services.

In many industrialized countries, spending and taxation by the government form a large portion of the nation's total economic activity. For example, total government spending in the United States equals about 40 percent of the nation's gross domestic product—that is, the value of all the goods and services produced within the United States in one year

History of Economic Thought

Economic issues have occupied people's minds since ancient times. Greek philosophers Aristotle and Plato wrote about problems of wealth, property, and trade. Both felt that to live by trade was undesirable. The Romans borrowed their economic ideas from the Greeks and showed the same contempt for trade.

During the Middle Ages (5ᵗʰ century to 15th century), the Roman Catholic Church condemned usury (the taking of interest for money loaned) and regarded commerce as inferior to agriculture.

The development of modern nationalism during the 16th century shifted economic attention to increasing the wealth and power of the various nation-states. The economic policy of the time was known as mercantilism. Mercantilists valued gold and silver because with these metals a ruler could hire and outfit mercenaries, thus increasing the country's power. Many European nations began colonizing other parts of the world and siphoning precious metals and raw materials from their colonies.

A school of thought known as physiocracy arose in France during the second half of the 18th century. The physiocrats believed that all wealth originates in agriculture; wealth is then distributed from farmers to other groups. The physiocrats promoted free trade and laissez-faire. British economist Adam Smith met the leading physiocrats and developed their doctrines in his writings.

As a coherent economic theory, classical economics starts with Smith, continues with British economists Thomas Robert Malthus and David Ricardo, and culminates with British economist John Stuart Mill. Classical economists agreed on several major principles. All believed in private property, free markets, and the benefits of competition. They shared Smith's suspicion of governmental involvement in the economy and his belief that the individual pursuit of private gain increased the public good. From Ricardo, classicists derived the notion of diminishing returns, which held that as more labor and capital were applied to land, a point was reached after which yields steadily diminished.

One debate was in regard to population growth. Malthus maintained that human population growth would eventually outstrip food production, leading to famine, war, epidemics, and plague. Mill believed that human population could rationally be limited. He also thought that government could play a role in the economy and favored worker ownership of factories. Mill thus represents a bridge between classical laissez-faire economics and an emerging welfare state.

German political philosopher Karl Marx provided the most important opposition to classical economics Marx's historical studies convinced him that profit and other property income result from force and fraud inflicted by the strong on the weak. Thus, the central social conflict is between capitalists who own the means of production—factories and machines—and workers who possess nothing but their bare hands. Exploitation is measured by the capacity of capitalists to pay no more than subsistence wages to their employees and extract for themselves as profit the difference between these wages and the selling price of market commodities. Marx argued that the internal contradictions within capitalism—its social inequities—would eventually end its existence.

According to Marx, the crises of capitalism would manifest themselves in falling rates of profit, mounting hostility between workers and employers, and ever more severe depressions. Class warfare would lead to revolution and progress toward, first, socialism and, ultimately, communism. Once communism was achieved, the state would wither away, and each individual would be compensated according to need.

Classical economics proceeded from the assumption of scarcity of resources. Dating from the 1870s, neoclassicist economists shifted emphasis from limitations on supply to interpretations of consumer choice. Neoclassicists explained market prices according to the intensity of consumer preference for one more unit of a commodity. British economist Alfred Marshall explained demand by the principle of marginal utility, and supply by the rule of marginal productivity (the cost of producing the last item of a given quantity). In competitive markets, consumer preferences for low prices of goods and seller preferences for high prices settle on a mutually agreeable level. This same reconciliation between supply and demand occurs in markets for money and human labor. For example, in competitive labor markets, actual wages represent to the employer the value of the output, and to the employee the acceptable compensation for the work.

During the Great Depression of the 1930s, accepted strategies for reversing the depression failed, and fresh policies were urgently required. British economist John Maynard Keynes supplied them. In his work, The General Theory of Employment, Interest, and Money (1936), he asserted that (1) neither high prices nor high wages explain persistent depression and mass unemployment, and (2) the explanation of these phenomena should be focused on aggregate demand—that is, the total spending of consumers, business investors, and governmental bodies. When aggregate demand is low, sales and jobs suffer; when it is high, all is well and prosperous. These ideas form the basis of contemporary macroeconomics. The national economy depends not on the actions of consumers, who are limited in the amounts that they can spend by the size of their incomes, but on business investors and governments, who invest in the economy. In a recession or depression, the proper thing to do is either to enlarge private investment or create public substitutes. This is done through easy credit or low interest rates, or more drastically by incurring deliberate budget deficits through public projects or subsidies to afflicted groups.

Economic Systems

The two major economic systems are the free-enterprise system and the Communist system. The major differences between these concern ownership of factories, farms, and other enterprises, and contrasting principles of pricing and income distribution. In free-enterprise societies, much of the gross national product (GNP) is directly generated by profit-making business enterprises, farmers, and private institutions.

Prices are determined by markets, and income is not firmly established. In Communist economies, the state plans much of the price setting, and there is public ownership of factories, farms, and large retail establishments. However, all organized economic systems mix market activity and government intervention to some degree.

Falling somewhere between societies that emphasize either central planning or free enterprise are those that formally practice social democracy, or liberal socialism. For example, Sweden organizes the bulk of productive activity under private ownership but regulates this activity closely, intervenes to protect the jobs of workers, and redistributes substantial portions of profits and large individual incomes to low-income groups.

Current Economic Problems

Between 1945 and 1973, the economies of the industrialized nations of Western Europe, Japan, and the United States grew rapidly. Several circumstances contributed to this, but perhaps the most important was that energy was plentiful and cheap. In the early 1970s, the Organization of Petroleum Exporting Countries (OPEC), which controls the bulk of the world's oil reserves, sharply raised its prices. This hampered economic growth worldwide. The heightened oil prices increased other product prices, leading to inflation and reduced purchasing power. This in turn depressed sales of consumer items, resulting in layoffs. Poorer nations had to borrow money, and their interest payments further slowed their development plans.

The various economic problems of recent years have stimulated serious debate about the proper role of public policy. Parties on the political left in

Europe advocated more controls and more planning. In the 1980s, a different solution was tried in the United States and the United Kingdom. Attempts were made to diminish taxation and government regulation on private enterprise and thus, by enlarging the potential profits of corporations, to encourage additional investment, higher productivity, and renewed economic growth. By the early 1990s, the fall of Communist governments in most of Eastern Europe underlined the trend away from centrally planned economies and toward a freer market system.

Public Goods

Governments provide public goods—government-financed items and services such as roads, military forces, lighthouses, and street lights. Private citizens would not voluntarily pay for these services, and therefore businesses have no incentive to produce them.

Public finance also enables governments to correct or offset undesirable side effects of a market economy. These side effects are called spillovers or externalities. For example, households and industries may generate pollution and release it into the environment without considering the adverse effect pollution has on others. If it costs less to pollute than not to, people and businesses have a financial incentive to continue polluting. Pollution is a spillover because it affects people who are not responsible for it.

To correct a spillover, governments can encourage or restrict certain activities. For example, governments can sponsor recycling programs to encourage less pollution, pass laws that restrict pollution, or impose charges or taxes on activities that cause pollution.

Public finance provides government programs that moderate the incomes of the wealthy and the poor. These programs include social security, welfare, and other social programs. For example, some elderly people or people with disabilities require financial assistance because they cannot work. Governments redistribute income by collecting taxes from their wealthier citizens to provide resources for their needy ones. The taxes fund programs that help support people with low incomes.

Public spending

Each year national, state, and local governments create a budget to determine how much money they will spend during the upcoming year. The budget determines which public goods to produce, which spillovers to correct, and how much assistance to provide to financially disadvantaged people. The chief administrator of the government—such as the president, prime minister, governor, or mayor—proposes the budget. However, the legislature—such as the congress, parliament, state legislature, or city council—ultimately must pass the budget. The legislature often changes the size and composition of the budget, but it must not make changes that the chief administrator will reject and veto.

Government spending takes two forms: exhaustive spending and transfer spending exhaustive spending refers to purchases made by a government for the production of public goods. For example, to construct a new harbor the government buys and uses resources from the economy, such as labor and raw materials. In transfer spending the government transfers income to people to help them support themselves.

Transfers can be one of two kinds: cash or in-kind. Cash transfers are cash payments, such as social security checks and welfare payments. In-kind transfers involve no cash payments but instead transfer goods or services to recipients. Examples of in-kind transfers include food stamp coupons and Medicare. Recipients of food stamp coupons exchange the coupons for groceries.

As recently as the 1960s, most spending by the U.S. government was exhaustive spending for items such as national defense, roads, airports, schools, and parks. In the mid-1960s transfer spending began to grow rapidly. In the United States today, over 50 percent of federal government spending is for cash and in-kind transfers. About 20 percent of state and local government spending is transfer spending.

Public Revenue

Governments must have funds, or revenue, to pay for their activities. Governments generate some revenue by charging fees for the services they provide, such as entrance fees at national parks or tolls for using a highway. However, most government revenue comes from taxes, such as income taxes, capital taxes, and sales and excise taxes.

An important source of tax revenue in most industrialized countries is the income or payroll tax, also known as the personal income tax. Income taxes are imposed on labor or activities that generate income, such as wages or salaries.

In the United States, income taxes account for about half of the total revenue of local, state, and federal governments combined. The federal government, many state governments, and some local governments levy personal income taxes.

Another important source of government revenue is the capital tax. Capital includes items or facilities that generate profits, such as factories, business machinery, and real estate. Some types of capital taxes are known as "profits" taxes. One kind of capital tax used by the federal government in the United States is the corporate income tax. A property tax is a capital tax used by state and local governments. Property taxes are levied on items such as houses or boats.

Sales and excise taxes are also a major source of government tax revenue. Many state and local governments levy a sales tax on the purchase of certain items. Consumers usually pay a percentage of the sales price as the tax. Excise taxes are used by all levels of government an excise tax is levied on a specific product, such as alcohol, cigarettes, or gasoline. The tax is usually included in the purchase price.

In Canada and many European, South American, and Asian countries, a value-added tax (VAT) provides significant revenue. The VAT is levied on the value added to a product during production as its components are assembled into final goods. For example, a clothing manufacturer might spend $500 on fabric, thread, zippers, and other goods required to make dresses. The manufacturer then adds $1000 to cover the costs of labor and the use of machines and equipment and sells the dresses for a total of $1500. The value-added tax is paid on this $1000.

Government spending and taxation directly affect the overall performance of the economy. For example, if the government increases spending to build a new highway, construction of the highway will create jobs. Jobs create income that people spend on purchases, and the economy tends to grow. The opposite happens when the government increases taxes. Households and businesses have less of their income to spend, they purchase fewer goods, and the economy tends to shrink. A government's fiscal policy is the way the government spends and taxes to influence the performance of the economy.

When the government spends more than it receives, it runs a deficit. Governments finance deficits by borrowing money. Deficit spending— that is, spending funds obtained by borrowing instead of taxation—can be helpful for the economy. For example, when unemployment is high, the government can undertake projects that use workers who would otherwise be idle.

The economy will then expand because more money is being pumped into it. However, deficit spending also can harm the economy. When unemployment is low, a deficit may result in rising prices, or inflation. The additional government spending creates more competition for scarce workers and resources and this inflates wages and prices.

The total of all federal government deficits forms the national debt. The size of the U.S. national debt has grown during the 20th century. The debt equaled about $25 billion in 1919 after World War I and about $260 billion in 1945 after World War II. In 1970, the debt stood at about $380 billion. Ten years later, the national debt had soared to nearly $1 trillion. In 1996 the national debt totaled about $5 trillion.

Final

Many people are concerned about the size of the U.S. national debt. They fear that a large amount of debt harms the economy and feel that the money used to pay interest on the debt could be better spent on other uses. Some people are also concerned about the ability of future generations to pay back the debt.

However, many economists argue that the size of the debt is misleading. They point out that an important measure of the severity of a nation's debt is its size as a percentage of the nation's gross domestic product. Based on this measurement, the national debt of the United States during the mid-1990s was about half the size of the U.S. debt at the end of World War II in 1945.

Other economists contend that when the balance of the debt is compared between years it does not account for the effects of inflation, which makes balances from later years appear larger.

Chapter 7

The Communist Manifesto

The story of the Manifesto is often interpreted differently. It is a story of capitalism, it is a story of the bourgeois and it is a story of revolution. It is a story with many facets, political, cultural and ideological progress pitted against material and economic development. It is a story of the past and quite possibly a story of the future but it is not a story of the total abatement of capitalism.

Capitalism and democracy can exist hand in hand because capitalism control labor because the people have the right to market their labor, not because capitalism factors owners and businessmen have any exclusive political rights but because the people have a right. This is the rot to why Great Britain did not erupt in all revolution in 1848 and it is the rot to why capitalism countries are still prospering which communist countries are succumbing to their own inadequacies.

In 1999 the world will observe the 151 anniversary of the publication of "The Communist Manifesto" by Karl Marx and Fredrich Engels. Both men were revolutionary German political theorist. Marx, of course, was one of the most renown political thinkers of his time.

His views influenced not only the philosophy of the time but the everyday workings as well. These views would eventually be classified under the title "Marxism" and would serve to shape socialism and communism and indeed to influence the political, economic and social history of the world. Much controversy often arises around the interpretation of the Manifesto. Much of this controversy centers around what is perceived as the Manifesto's ideas regarding capitalism.

Although many interpret the target of the Manifesto as being capitalism as a whole this is not exactly the case.

The Manifesto was a production of a specific time period and social and economic stage, a stage which was set to a large degree pre-capitalism in Western Europe. "The Communist Manifest" is simply that, a manifesto.

It is neither lengthy or detailed yet it is quite possibly the most influential example of political writing since the Eighteenth Century and the French Revolution.

The term "manifesto" is defined as a public declaration of policy or opinion. The Manifesto is simply a dramatic statement of the authors purpose. It was a call to arms for the lower classes to rise up in rebellion against the upper classes.

The projections found in the Manifesto are truly impressive regarding the future of capitalism. In the Manifesto Britain may indeed have served as the model of the capitalistic system which Marx and Engel so carefully analyze but it is clear in reviewing the work that this was not the inspiration for the story of the bourgeoisie[1] acting as a revolutionary political force.

The Manifesto portrays the bourgeois class as one of continual struggle, first oppressed by the feudal aristocracy and then eventually evolving, with much effort, to the modern representative state.

The Manifesto makes it clear that every step of the way the bourgeois was dependent on the aid of the working classes and eventually the modern proletariat[1] for its advances. This, in turn, presented the working class with the weapons needed to enact its own revolution against the bourgeois.

Another point that is relevant to the changes which were to come was the bequeathal by the bourgeois to the working classes the ideas of the Enlightenment. Not only did this ideology enlighten, it empowered.

Capitalism is very much a part of the story of the Manifesto it serves as a progressive force for revolution. It is not, however, the only force or even the primary focus of Marx's work.

The demands of the Manifesto are quite simple in that it called for an overthrow of the middle class (the bourgeoisie), a change in the power structure of the time to allow rule by the working class (the proletariat) and the termination of class-based society. The Manifesto demanded communal property in the place of private property, a completely different prospect for the status quo of the day where the lives of the commoners.

---

[1] By bourgeoisie is meant the class of modern capitalists, owners of the means of social production and employers of wage-labor. By proletariat, the class of modern wage-laborers who, having no means of productions of their own, are reduced to selling they're labor-power in order to live. (Note by Engels in English Edition of 1888)

This called for the rents collected from properties to be applied to public purposes and no longer allowed the concept of inheritance or even the private ownership of factories and other places of production.

The Manifesto also allowed for considerable benefits to children including free education and the abolition of child labor in factories.

It is not the actual wording of the Manifesto which has stirred so much controversy, it is the various interpretations of that wording and the impact those interpretations have had at various times on societies around the world. The Manifesto has been viewed not only as a uniquely influential political document but also as a work of history and an economic, political and cultural analysis.

Indeed it has been viewed as a prophesy, not only as an account of the past and present but as an account of the future which has yet to unfold. In this interpretation the Manifesto becomes not only a document of extreme importance to the times in which it was written but also a document of extreme importance to the present and the future of societies all over the world.

The question arises with the Manifesto as to how exactly such a small and seemingly innocuous format, what really amounts to a small pamphlet written by two relatively young men of one and one-half centuries ago, can have such an impact on the modern world of political philosophy. The Manifesto has such an impact simply because of its format, its authors, and the times and political arena in which it was written (Wood, 1998). Nineteenth century Western Europe was characterized by the emergence of industrial capitalism and a corresponding industrial working class.

From these working classes would grow working class movements which would become powerful political forces in Western Europe complete with socialist parties and socialist literature. The Manifesto comprised only a portion of this literature. Marx and Engel were joined by writers such as Owen, St. Simon, and Fourier, all of whom presented similar socialist views. It just so happened that the Manifest would become the more better-known of these publications.

The Manifesto was more systematic and to the point than the other socialist writings of the day. It attacked capitalism head-on in a manner which had never been attempted before, providing a critical analysis which complemented its urgings for rebellion. Part of the reason for its distinction from the other socialist writings of the day was that it had been commissioned by the German Communist League in 1847. As shall be seen, capitalism would not be the primary target of the Manifesto nor would one of the most progressive capitalist countries of the time be significantly affected by its content.

It was actually Friedrich Engels (age twenty-seven) who drafted the Principles of Communism. These were then handed over the Karl Marx (age twenty-nine) for revision. The final product became the theoretical and literary masterpiece that we know today. The Manifesto was first published in London anonymously in 1848.

The publication would accompany the widespread revolution which was already sweeping across Europe from France to Germany to Hungary to Italy and beyond (Wood, 1998). The revolution of the time affected areas which today are encompassed by ten different European countries. As those effects weren't enough others were felt in countries as far away as Latin America.

Within just a few short weeks the fall of one government was followed by the fall of many. The impact of these revolutions were not limited to their actual effect but also to their anticipated effect. International revolution was anticipated as it had been at no other time in history.

Many point to the Manifesto itself as the root of the wide scale revolution of 1848 but in reality the document was a product of the time period and events which spawned the revolution, not a cause of the revolution itself.

As a product of the same time period and philosophical thought which led the widespread revolution of 1848 the Manifesto has inherent strengths and weaknesses (Wood, 1998). The countries in which revolution erupted were not mirror images of one another, if fact they were extremely diverse both socially, economically and politically.

Revolution occurred in more developed countries such as France and parts and Germany just as it did in the lesser developed countries such as southern Italy and Transylvania. Most of the countries which would succumb to revolution had significant rural populations.

Interestingly, these countries had another commonality, the fact that capitalism was not that advanced in any of them. Britain, perhaps, was one of the most progressive in terms of capitalism preceding the great European revolution of 1848. It can be questioned why revolution failed to erupt on the same scale in Britain as it did in many of the other countries in Europe. Britain more so than any other country should have been ripe for revolution given the concepts of the Manifesto and other socialist thought of the day. From the middle part of the 1700s to through the early half of the 1800s, the period known as the Industrial Revolution, Great Britain was quickly transitioning from a subsistence pattern which involved primarily agricultural pursuits to one which depended almost solely on complex machinery and rather than the simpler hand tools which had characterized her earlier history.

Modern scholars question why Great Britain was the first country to experience the Industrial Revolution. Although there are numerous speculations, one of the most probable is that the capital and credit markets in Great Britain were sufficient to support the creation of new industry when it was needed. It is quite possibly this same ability which insulated Britain from the widespread revolution which would eventually occur in other European countries. The economic situation in Great Britain allowed the ability to build the factories and to outfit them with the needed machinery at a time which corresponded with societal need. Few, if any, other countries in the world had the critical economic support, access to raw materials and market in the latter part of the 1700s.

Another factor which entered the picture was in the philosophies of the people. Eighteenth and nineteenth century British were questioning many of the basic premises of life and how they related to that life.

Many facets of British society would change with the Industrial Revolution. Masses of people who had previously worked out their livelihoods in agricultural pursuits migrated to the cities to take up employment in the great factories which were opening their doors.

Factory employment provided The British with more disposable income and allowed them to enjoy, at least to some extent, some of the niceties of life. Although there was admittedly a clear separation between economic classes, this separation was not felt to the extent that it was in other European countries. With this enjoyment came the impetus to make greater and greater economic leaps through the avenue of industry. One invention followed another and the lifestyles of the common peoples changed more than they had at any other time in history.

Some authors notes that it wasn't a single invention or innovation but rather an accumulation of developments which allowed Europe in general and England specifically to differentiate itself from the rest of the world in terms of exponential economic growth.

There were also conflicts which came apparent in the philosophical component of the British people during the Industrial Revolution. The sudden transition of seventeenth century values into eighteenth century values was almost overnight. What the eighteenth century held in high esteem the nineteenth century shunned. During the European revolutions of 1848 there was most certainly popular unrest and even state repression in Great Britain. In Britain, however, this unrest and discontent never resulted in the revolutionary upheaval experienced by much of Western Europe. The author of the article "The Communist Manifesto after 150 years", Ellen Melksins Wood observes:

"There was a mass political movement in Britain too, the Chartist movement, but its political struggles (for instance, the struggle for an extension of the franchise to the working class, which would be won some time later) were being overtaken by new kinds of class struggle. The growth of industrial capitalism was already shifting the central terrain of class conflict from the political arena to the workplace, the point of production".

So it seems that the concepts of the Manifesto were not one-hundred percent applicable in Great Britain. Perhaps even more interestingly, they were not even one-hundred percent applicable in much of the rest of Western Europe where revolution did occur. This illuminates the fact that the various revolutions did have a common political program but that this program was not the overthrow of capitalism but instead the establishment of unified liberal or constitutional states in which civil equality was given high importance.

The quest to find a better way was undoubtedly inspired in Western Europe by the French Revolution of the previous century. Many of the concepts contained in the Manifesto were undoubtedly inspired by this revolution as well. The French Revolution, 1789-1799, ended the absolute power of the monarchy and introduced many democratic reforms to France but it did not make France a democracy. French law decried that the population be divided into three divisions called estates. The first estate was comprised of the clergy, the second group was the nobles and the third was made of the rest of the people. The third group was predominantly peasant but this class also included the working people of the cities and a sizable middle class which were prosperous and were lawyers, merchants and government officials.

France was trying to finance two wars and was on the verge of bankruptcy. This was putting greater financial burden on the third estate. New ideas opposing the absolute authority of the king were becoming more popular and widespread. Some people believed that the power to rule should come from the people.

The classes which existed in France in the latter 1700s had been in existence for several hundred years but there was no mobility among the divisions. This led to resentment from the peasant and prosperous middle class. The nobles and clergy paid no taxes therefore the peasants, who could least afford it, and the prosperous middle class were financing the government. The middle class resented the lack of prestige due to their class and the fact that they could not change classes. This of course resulted in revolution.

With the rise of Napoleon, however, the French Revolution came to an end. Although there had been many changes there would still be discontent and in 1848 revolution would raise its head once again. The economic, social, and political situation which existed in France during the

1800s would mirror the concepts outlined in the Manifesto. The same could be said of countries such as Italy, Hungary, and the other countries of Western Europe which would ultimately experience revolution in 1848. The situations leading up to revolution grew from a great chasm between the masses of working people and the ruling monarchs and aristocracy. The labors of the masses were directed to maintaining an extremely affluent lifestyle of the very few while the workers themselves remained in miserable conditions.

Although capitalism was the strongest in Britain during this time period, Britain would be the least affected by the revolutions of 1848 and it is here where the concepts outlined in the Manifesto fall short in accurately describing the need and avenue for revolution.

Although the concepts enumerated in the Manifesto fell short of explaining why Great Britain, the center of capitalism of the time in Western Europe, was not engulfed in revolution as were other Western European countries; these concepts were accurate in many regards. The true revolutionary movement results in change to the status quo of a system. A revolution is an evolutionary process whereby challenges to the system develop to a critical point after which there is a period of searching for stability within the new system. This would occur in most of the countries which found themselves entangled in the revolutions of 1848.

What the revolutions of 1848 were not was a socialist or anti-capitalist revolution. Neither were they a "bourgeoisie revolution" as would be suggested by the premises of the Manifesto. We can say that the "bourgeois" of the time was not a coherent capitalist class. Instead it consisted of civil servants, professionals and intellectuals. In the more industrialized countries the bourgeois was a small and relatively weak opposing force to the dominant regime.

As such it was incapable of acting alone and dependent on the support of popular forces with different material interest in the opposition of the ruling elite. In reality it was these "popular forces", composed of the unemployed or underemployed, independent craftsmen, small shopkeepers, and peasants alike, who would fight and die in the streets. They were not a modern mass proletariat. In fact, a large organized proletariat was not present anywhere in revolutionary Europe. This had not been the case in Britain where a sizable class of wage-laborers were employed by the capitalist system. What this meant in revolutionary Europe is that the revolutions indeed erupted but in effect failed in that no single class had the strength, organization, and numbers necessary to sustain a stable regime of its own.

In the Manifesto it is apparent that the supposed revolutionary hero is the bourgeoisie. The Manifesto did not predict a socialist revolution or a proletarian revolution, however, but it did give hope that revolution would erupt which would have long term consequences and which would surpass the bourgeois republic and result in proletarian rule and eventually socialism. Although the Manifesto serves as a call to arm for the working class and indeed recognizes that class as the true revolutionary force it is the story of the bourgeoisie triumph.

The Manifesto addresses the capitalism which was prevalent in the mid-nineteenth century, not an advanced form of capitalism by any means. The emphasis of the Manifesto, however, is against a social situation which erupted prior to the emergence of even that level of capitalism (Wood, 1998). It is true that capitalism was the target as well but Marx and Engels were really concerned with pre-capitalist formations more so than capitalist social relations. Here is where the various interpretations of the Manifesto are sometimes inaccurate and generate controversy.

The true emphasis of the Manifesto is non-privileged against privileged, not wage-laborer against capitalist employers. True, the Manifesto is a manifesto of communism and proletarian revolution against capitalism.

Chapter 8

Brazilian Impeachment Procedures Vs.
U.S. Impeachment Procedures

The concept of impeachment arose in the second half of the 19th century in Great Britain. It was initially conceived as an instrument of parliamentary oversight of the executive and was designed to hold those exercising political power accountable both individually and for administrative acts of the State. In England, the House of Commons, *the most solemn grand inquest of the whole kingdom*, is charged with formulating the accusation, while the House of Lords, *the most high and supreme Court of Criminal Jurisdiction of the kingdom*, sits in judgement.

The power of judgment exercised by the House of Lords is not restricted to political crimes but is also extensive to criminal offenses, thus justifying the fact that it has issued sentences normally reserved to the criminal court system, including banishment and even capital punishment.

Though initially targeted at government ministers, impeachment could also, at least in thesis, be used against all subjects of the kingdom and seems to have been applied to judges and jurists. In the 1678 judgement of Lord Danby, it was determined that Ministers were accountable not only for questions of legality, but also for honesty, fairness and the usefulness of their acts.

The United States of America was the legitimate heir to the English concept of impeachment. That nation rapidly adapted the institution of impeachment to its own needs and incorporated it into the system of checks and balances among the three branches of government, an essential element of any federal system. Aside from this, the United States transformed it into an essentially political instrument. Though the question is not dealt with in the Articles of Confederation, the colonies of Virginia, New Jersey, Delaware, Pennsylvania, Maryland, North Carolina, Georgia and New York introduced the concept of impeachment into the debates at the Philadelphia Convention.

Aside from the President and Vice President, all civil servants in the United States are subject to impeachment. In the American Constitution, impeachment is cited in article I, Section 3; article II, Section 4; and article III, Section 3. Article II, Section 4 states the following: *"The President, Vice President and all Civil Officers of the United States, shall be removed from Office on Impeachment for, and Conviction of, Treason, Bribery, or other high Crimes and Misdemeanors"*.

The fundamental difference between impeachment in England and in the United States is the fact that, in the first case, the House of Lords has full and unlimited jurisdiction to judge the accused, even for criminal acts, and can apply sanctions of a penal nature to the accused. In the United States, on the other hand, the only punishment that the Senate can impose is removal from office and ineligibility for office, while the Judiciary is responsible for judging any common crimes that may have been committed.

Another important difference is that, in the case of the House of Lords, impeachment trials are not carried out under oath, though each member will make what is called a declaration of honor. In contrast to this, the members of the American Senate, when brought together in a Court of Impeachment, are placed under oath.

In Brazil, the institution of impeachment is very similar to the American model, particularly in the sense that, in both countries, the only sanctions that the Senate can impose are removal from office and ineligibility, while the Judiciary is charged with judging common crimes and imposing the corresponding sanctions. Consequently, in Brazil, the process of impeachment is also an essentially political proceeding.

IMPEACHMENT IN BRAZIL

In Brazilian constitutional law, the expression *"crimes of responsibility"* corresponds to political-administrative violations not subject to penalties of a criminal nature. On committing *"crimes of responsibility"*, the public agent violates the duties inherent to his public position or function.

In Brazil, impeachment is defined in the Federal Constitution and in Ordinary Law no. 1,079, dated 04.10.50[3]. These instruments grant the Federal Senate exclusive authority to judge the President and Vice President of the Republic for crimes of responsibility, as well as Ministers of State for crimes of the same nature connected to those said to have been committed by the President or Vice President, and the Ministers of the Federal Supreme Court, Attorney General of the Republic and the Chief Federal Legal Advisor.

---

[3] Law approved by simple majority vote of the National Congress (See art 59, III).

The Brazilian Senate is composed of 81 members or three from each state and the Federal District and their tenure in office is eight years. Every four years, the representation of each state and the Federal District is renewed alternately by one third and two thirds of the members.

Governors, mayors and the members of municipal councils are also subject to impeachment for crimes of responsibility. However, these trials are not held before the Federal Senate.

The Governors of the States and Federal District are judged by their respective Assemblies or as determined in the state constitutions. Normally, once the required authorization has been granted by the Assembly or Legislative Chamber[4], Governors are judged by a mixed tribunal composed of 5 State Deputies and 5 Senior Judges[5], with the Senior Judge who holds the position of President of the Court of Justice of the State or Federal District as the presiding judge. The members of the court of impeachment are chosen as follows: the representatives of the legislature are elected by the full Assembly or Chamber, while those from the Judiciary are chosen by lot.

Mayors and Councilpersons are judged by the Municipal Legislative Chambers, according to the terms of Decree Law no. 201, dated February 27, 1967. In these cases, there is a basic difference that deserves mention. When judging mayors and councilpersons, the powers of the respective legislative councils are restricted to removal from office and do not include loss of political rights or ineligibility for public office. However, article 1,

---

[4] In the states, the legislatures are called Legislative Assemblies in contrast to the Federal District, where the legislature is called the Legislative Chamber.

[5] Known as "Desembargadores" in Brazil, these are senior judges who render judgements as a collegial body.

l, line "b" of Complementary Law 64/90, states that office-holders who have been found guilty are ineligible for election during the remaining period of the mandate for which that person was originally elected and in the three year period subsequent to the end of that legislature.

If there is no consistent connection or link between the crime of responsibility practiced by the President or Vice President and the crime practiced by a Minister of State, the latter will be judged by the Federal Supreme Court, the highest court of the judicial system, and not by the Federal Senate. Consequently, one concludes that crimes of responsibility committed exclusively by Ministers of State will always be judged by the Supreme Court and not by the Senate.[6]

In this paper, we will analyze the process of impeachment before the Brazilian Federal Senate, with the objective of comparing it to the American impeachment process which, as is well known, is a function reserved to that country's Senate. Consequently, we will not deal with the impeachment of Brazilian Governors, Mayors and Councilpersons.

The Brazilian Constitution was promulgated on 10.05.88 by a Constituent Assembly convoked specifically for this purpose. In the paragraph of article 85, the Brazilian Constitution states that crimes of responsibility committed by the President of the Republic *"will be defined in special legislation".*

Since, according to the grammar of the Portuguese language, the verb "will be" above is in the future tense, it was understood that, once the Federal Constitution had been promulgated, the National Congress would meet with the objective of approving special legislation containing a definition of

---

[6] Brazilian Federal Constitution, article 52, l.

crimes of responsibility, as required by the provision in article 85, paragraph, of the Federal Constitution. However, this was not done.

On September 23, 1992, the Brazilian Supreme Court issued a surprising decision in a case designated Appeal no. 21,564[7], involving the interpretation of the paragraph of article 85 of the Federal Constitution. The Court stated that, despite the future tense of the verb in the Constitution, for purposes of impeachment proceedings and the definition of crimes of responsibility, there is no impediment to application of Law no. 1,079, passed by the Congress on 04.10.50, more than 48 years prior to promulgation of the Federal Constitution.

The decision issued by the Supreme Court was all the more surprising in the sense that, once he has been considered guilty[8], the punishment to be imposed on the President of the Republic is defined in the Federal Constitution (article 52, paragraph), while the crime upon which the accusation is based is that specified in a lesser law promulgated more than 48 years ago or, more precisely, in article 5 to 10 of Law no. 1,079, dated 04.10.50. Thus, we have the following situation: the crimes upon which the accusation is based are defined in less important legislation approved by a simple majority of the Congress, while the sanctions are specified in the nation's constitution.

Consequently, once the Chief Federal Legal Advisor is excluded, all other public agents to be tried before the Federal Senate will be judged according to the terms of Law no. 1,079/50.

---

[7] According to the Brazilian Constitution, the term used for this instrument is *"Mandado de Segurança"* or a court-issued injunction.

[8] When found guilty, the punishment imposed on the President of the Republic is removal from office and ineligibility for public office for a period of eight years.

Here, one should stress that the office of the Chief Federal Legal Advisor is excluded for the simple reason that this position, which corresponds to the chief legal advisor of the President of the Republic, was introduced with the 1988 Constitution and, therefore, did not exist when Law no. 1,079/50 was passed. Though the Brazilian Constitution was promulgated more than ten years ago, no legislation has been passed in the intervening period dealing with impeachment of the Chief Federal Legal Advisory. Thus, should he be charged with the crime of responsibility, there is no way in which, according to Brazilian legislation, he could possibly be tried before the Federal Senate or any other entity for that matter.

According to Law no. 1,079/50, any Brazilian citizen entitled to full civil and political rights is qualified to denounce a public authority before the Federal Senate. However, the denunciation must be received and examined while the accused has not definitively left office. Should the office be vacant for any reason whatsoever, including resignation or dismissal from office upon request, the process of impeachment cannot be initiated no matter what the gravity of the accusations.

In the case of the Ministers of the Federal Supreme Court and the Attorney General of the Republic, the denunciation is submitted directly to the Federal Senate with no need for examination by the Federal Chamber of Deputies. In this specific case, there is no need for a Committee of Accusation, since the denouncing party would be called upon to sustain the accusation before the Senate.

In cases involving accusations against the President, Vice President and Ministers of State, the denunciation must first be submitted to the Federal Chamber of Deputies. That House of Congress is charged with examining the denunciation of crimes of responsibility and determining whether it is or is not admissible. The members of the full House are called individually by name and must announce their acceptance or rejection of the denunciation. During this stage of the process, the accused is not entitled to defense, since the House is not sitting in judgment of the accused but rather deciding whether or not there are grounds for a trial.

Once the denunciation has been accepted by two thirds of the Chamber of Deputies, the entire process, including the accusation and all other documents appended by the accusing party, are remitted to the Federal Senate where the accused will be tried. At that point, the Chamber of Deputies designates a Commission of Accusation composed of three Federal Deputies who are charged with accompanying the process before the Senate. This Commission will present the formal accusation before the Senate and define the limits of the denunciation. Once the case has come before the Federal Senate, article 23, § 4 of Law no. 1,079/50 excludes the accusing party (citizen) from the process and charges the aforementioned Commission with exclusive responsibility for presenting the charges.

The processing of an impeachment before the Federal Senate is more or less the same no matter who is being judged. According to Brazilian law, there are two distinct phases to the process before the Senate: 1) *judicium accusationis* (judgment of the accusation); 2) *judicium causae* (the judgment itself).

During the entire impeachment process, the accused, the Commission of Accusation and the Senators are entitled to contest any witness brought forward by either side. This can be done by casting doubt upon the testimony of witnesses, raising suspicions as to their reliability or possible impediments to acceptance of their testimony or even raising the possibility of false witness.

However, the accused is not permitted to question the reliability or possible impediments involving the Senators who are to sit in judgement.

Consequently, according to the decision taken by the Brazilian Supreme Court in the case of appeal no. 21,623, dated December 17, 1992[9], there is nothing to stop a Senator who is already under suspicion for one reason or another or even subject to impediment from participating normally in the judgment and voting to find the accused guilty as charged.

When the accusation is submitted to the Federal Senate, in another or even subject to impediment from participating normally in the judgment and voting the accused guilty as charged.

When the accusation is submitted to the Federal Senate, in cases involving Ministers of the Supreme Court or the Attorney General of the Republic, or when the accusatory documents are remitted to the Senate by the Chamber of Deputies, in cases involving the President, Vice President and Ministers of State, the Senate organizes a panel of seven members who are charged with accepting or rejecting the accusation.[10] The accused may appeal to the full Senate against any decisions taken by the Panel.

Once the accusations have been accepted by the Federal Senate, the denunciation and the principal documents are read in Plenary Session. Having concluded the reading of the documents, a Special Commission is created and is composed of representatives of the different parties in proportion to their representation in the Senate. The task of this Commission is to name a chairperson and secretary within 48 hours and then analyze the accusations. Within a period of ten days,[11] as of the formation of this Commission, it must issue its report which will be

---

[9] According to the Brazilian Constitution, the term used for this instrument is *"Mandado de Segurança"* or a court-issued injunction.

[10] Art. 44 of Law no. 1,079/50.

[11] Should there be a need for gathering evidence or taking statements, an additional 10 (ten) days may be allotted to the Special Commission.

published in the Official Gazette and printed in separate copies for distribution to the Senators.

Once the report is published, it is submitted to a full session of the Senate for discussion and a single round of voting in which the Senators are called upon by name to state their votes. Should the report be rejected, the process is considered null and the documents are placed on file. Should the report be accepted by a *simple majority* of votes, the process of impeachment goes forward and the accusation is placed in debate in the full Senate.

At this point, even before the defense is given the opportunity to state its position, the accused is suspended from the function he holds and, until the final sentence is issued, is subject to the loss of 1/3 of his wages.[12] At this point, the presidency of the impeachment proceedings is transferred to the President of the Federal Supreme Court. Should the accused be the President of the Republic, the Vice President is called upon to assume the Presidency of the Republic.

After having approved the Report issued by the Special Commission, the President of the Federal Supreme Court notifies the accused and, for the first time, calls upon him to present his defense which may include any type of evidence permitted by law, including witnesses, documentary evidence and expert testimony. Aside from this, the accused is allowed to interrogate, re-interrogate, contest, offer testimony and demand that he be placed face-to-face with his accusers.

The accused has a period of five days in which to appeal to the President of the Federal Supreme Court, as president of the impeachment proceedings,

---

[12] Law no. 1,079/50, art. 57, line "c".

with respect to the deliberations of the Special Commission. Should a period of one hundred and eighty days elapse without concluding the impeachment process, the President of the Republic–in those cases in which he is the accused–is returned to office though the process is not interrupted.[13]

Together with the notification suspending the accused from the position he occupies, the figure in question is also called upon to respond to the accusations within a period of twenty days, should he desire to do so. From the viewpoint of the law, it is at this moment in which the accused receives notification that the process of impeachment truly begins.

If the accused is not then within the area of the Federal District (the political-administrative seat of government), he will be notified personally by the President of the Court of Justice of the State in which he is located. Should he be abroad or in an unknown locality, this fact will be verified by the 1ˢᵗ Secretary of the Federal Senate, and the accused will be informed by notification published in the Official Gazette to appear before the Senate within the next sixty days to receive due notification. Within this period, once the accused has come before the Senate, he will have a period of twenty days in which to present his defense.

Having initiated the process of impeachment, the Special Commission will decide whether it will be necessary to interrogate the accused or not. Despite being notified officially by the Special Commission, it is the right of the accused not to be present at this stage of the process and to refuse to respond to any questions that may be formulated.

When the Commission of Accusation and the accused have concluded the period for producing evidence, the two sides will have successive periods of

---

[13] See article 86, § 2.

five days in which to present their final written allegations before the Special Commission.

Independently of whether they decide to present final allegations or not, the Special Commission will then have a period of ten days in which to issue another report, in which it will state its position as to whether the accusations are or are not well-founded. This report, together with all of the documents appended to it, is then published in the Official Gazette and distributed to the Senators. This is the stage known as *"the phase of arraignment"*.

After concluding, publishing and distributing the second report issued by the Special Commission, it is placed in discussion and put to a vote in a plenary session of the Federal Senate. At that point, the Senators must decide the following: 1) should the Senate understand that the accusations are not well-grounded, the entire process is terminated; 2) if the Senate approves the report by a *simple majority* of votes, the accusations are considered well-founded.

When voting is concluded, the accused, the accusing party and the Commission of Accusation, in those cases in which the Commission exists, are notified of the Senate's decision.

In the next step of the process, the accusing party and the Commission of Accusation–in cases involving the President, Vice President of the Republic and Ministers of State–are notified to come before the full Senate on the trial date to plead their case and call their witnesses.

After the defense has concluded its presentation, the records are sent to the President of the Federal Supreme Court who will schedule the date for judgment of the accused and notify the parties and witnesses at least ten days prior to that date.

Once the trial itself has been initiated, the parties are convoked and they may participate personally or through duly constituted representatives. If neither the accused nor his representative is present, the court decrees that the accused will be tried *in absentia* and appoints a court lawyer to defend the accused. At that point, another day is set for the trial.

The President of the Federal Supreme Court presides at the trial and all of the Senators present participate as judges. The first order of business is to read the records of the case and then question any witnesses that may have been called by the accusation and defense. Questions may be asked by the parties directly involved and by the Senators and are always channeled through the President of the impeachment court.

When the questioning of witnesses has terminated, oral debate begins and lasts for a period stipulated by the President of the court. The accusation is first to speak, followed by the defense. The accusation may reply and the defense is permitted to present its rejoinders.

Once the debates have been concluded, the President of the impeachment court will go back over the case and present a summary of the basic points raised by the accusation and defense and cite the evidence introduced during the proceedings. He will then call upon the Senators present by name and each one of them must then respond "Yes" of "No" to the following question: *"did the accused commit the crimes attributed to him and should the accused be sentenced to the loss of his position and temporary ineligibility to perform a public function?"*

The accused is found guilty if two thirds of the votes of the Federal Senate are affirmative.

Should the accused be found guilty, he is removed from office and is temporarily ineligible for the exercise of a public function. The period of ineligibility varies according to the office held by the person being tried.

When the President of the Republic is found guilty, ineligibility is set invariably at 8 (eight) years. For other public agents, such as Ministers of the Federal Supreme Court and the Attorney General of the Republic, ineligibility can be no greater than five years. In other words, in these cases, ineligibility can be set at anything between one day and five years.

Another point that deserves underlining is the fact that the ineligibility applicable to the President of the Republic is specified in the Federal Constitution, while the penalties applicable to other authorities are specified in ordinary legislation approved by a simple majority of votes.

CRITIQUE OF THE BRAZILIAN IMPEACHMENT PROCESS

The most severe criticism that one can level at the Brazilian system of impeachment is the understanding that the accused is not allowed to argue that the Senators themselves, who are the true judges of the impeachment process, may well not be impartial, may be under suspicion or, for one reason or another, should be impeded from voting. The basis of this understanding is the decision issued by the Federal Supreme Court with respect to appeal no. 21,623[14], which states that the Senators are not required to show the same characteristic of impartiality demanded of members of the Judiciary since, as members of parliament, they are affiliated to political parties and this is a circumstance incompatible with impartiality and independence.

In a process that results in Federal Senate application of a sanction of the highest gravity, in the sense that it restricts a fundamental right of a

---

[14] This type of appeal is called a "Mandado de Segurança", a type of court-issued injunction.

citizen, it is unthinkable not to demand that those sitting in judgment be impartial in their decisions. If a judge were not required to show impartiality, there would be no due process of law. In much the same way, there is no due process when the accused is not allowed to demonstrate the partiality of the judge.

Prof. Joseph Story, a former judge of the American Supreme Court is clear in this regard, in his work: *"A Familiar Exposition of the Constitution of the United States"*, pages 101, 102 and 112:

> "§§ 113. *The great objects to be attained in the selection of a tribunal for the trial of impeachment, are impartiality, integrity, intelligence and independence. If either of these qualities is wanting, the trial is essentially defective. To insure impartiality, the body must be, in some degree, removed from popular power and passions, from the influence of sectional prejudices, and from the still more dangerous influence of party spirit. To secure integrity, there must be a lofty sense of duty, and a deep responsibility to God, as well as to future ages".*

In keeping with the lesson put forward by Prof. Joseph Story, article 8 of the American Convention of Human Rights assures every citizen of the right to be tried by an ***independent and impartial*** judge or court. Precisely the same thing is required in article X of the Universal Declaration of Human Rights of 1949: *"Every person is entitled to a fair and public hearing in circumstances of full equality before an **independent and impartial** court in order to decide as to that person's rights or the grounds of any criminal accusation against that person".*

Another criticism that cannot be ignored is that, even before the accused is permitted to present his defense, he is suspended from his functions with a 30% reduction in wages. Since the principle of *due process of law* is based on the right of the accused to present his defense as fully as possible, it is certainly not advisable that the accused be suspended from office and subjected to a salary reduction even before being given any opportunity whatsoever to state his defense.

Another important point is the fact that, in most cases, the accusation before the Federal Senate is normally presented by the accusing party, making it clear that this can often lead to self-promotion under a limelight that is national in scope and even a private and personal vendetta against a public figure before the Senate.

In the Brazilian system, all trial sessions are public instead of secret. This circumstance opens the doors to media intervention, live national transmission of trial sessions, violations of the independence that Senators should demonstrate as the judges of the impeachment process, making them wary of voter reaction to their votes in the impeachment process. In the end, the Senators tend to give into outside pressures, with little or no attention to the facts as they are stated in the records. Their votes become questions of convenience, particularly since they are not under oath nor—as was already stressed—are they obligated to show impartiality and independence.

In the Brazilian impeachment system, when the President is accused he is automatically suspended from office before he is given any opportunity to present his defense. The Vice President of the Republic takes over as President. However, in cases in which the Vice President belongs to another party, as is common in Brazil, the Senators who are members of the Vice President's party may well be tempted to vote for the removal of the President as an unconventional and indirect way of attaining power without the need for facing voters. Once the President has been found guilty, the Vice President is proclaimed President until the next presidential election.

Another point that deserves criticism concerns the period of ineligibility. In the case of the President of the Republic, the period is invariably 8 years, while other authorities are subject to periods that may vary between one day and five years. The essential incoherence of this situation is evident in the following example: if the President is found guilty, the period of ineligibility to which he is automatically subject is eight years, no more no less. However, should the Vice President be found guilty of the same crimes while exercising the same functions, the period of ineligibility may vary from one day to a maximum of five years. At least from the legal-scientific point of view, there is no way in which this difference in sanctions for like crimes can possibly be justified.

Finally, The Brazilian impeachment process is totally incoherent when it defines the crimes of responsibility of the President of the Republic in ordinary legislation, approved by a simple majority of votes, while the sanctions to be applied to a President found guilty are defined in the Federal Constitution. In summary, the crime is defined in a less important law and the sanction in a law of much higher stature (the Federal Constitution).

About the Author

Rony Curvelo is the Special Assistant and Press Aid for the former Brazilian President since 1995. Born in Brazil, hold as well a U.S. citizenship. He received his bachelor degree in Public Administration from La Salle University and his certification in journalist from the University of Miami. Among others academic experiences, Mr. Curvelo has participated in the following seminars: Globalization and International Trade Seminar at the New Mexico University-Albuquerque-NM, American and Brazilian Constitution Seminar at the Free Interchange for the National Center of Laws—Tucson-AZ, Strategy Research in the Latin Countries Seminar, Miami-FL, "Brazilian/American Diplomacy" at the President John Quincy Institute, Quincy City-MA.

His previously experiences come from TV News broadcast anchor for BTN-Brazilian Television Network, News reporter for CBS-TeleNotícias, Free lancer News Reporter for CNN-Spanish, Host for the TV Manchete from Brazil, and News reporter for Univision.

Working with Mr. President Collor, he was responsible for the day to day administration of the Collor's office and for coordinating the administration between USA office and Brazil's office. In addition he has been the front line for dealing with the office's public relations in Brazil, The United States and others countries in Europe. Has travel to several countries to developed, promoted and produced several projects with non-governmental organizations as well as worked on lectures and speeches with universities, trade associations, and political groups. As press aid he has coordinated the press relation, developed videos, news releases and speaking engagement.

Most recently he was the Press Aid for the Mr. Collor Major campaign for the city of São Paulo.

Bibliography

1. Anthony Downs-Inside Bureaucracy-1994

2. Anonymous (1999, January 29). Watchdog says Cuba detains journalists, rights activists. Reuters, p. PG.

3. Anonymous (1996, June 20). Cuba approves only restricted Net access. Reuter's, at http://www.eff.org/pub/Censorship/GII_NII/Dispatches/cuba.062196.txt.

4. Brian J. Cook-Bureaucracy and Self-Government: Reconsidering the Role of The Public Administration in America Politics-1996

5. Charles H. Levine, B. Guy Peters, Frank J. Thompson-Public Administration, Challenges, Choices, Consequences-1990

6. Dirk Kruijt-The Hidden Crisis in Development : Development Bureaucracies–1996

7. Ferguson, Amanda (1999, January). U.S. district court declares filters on all library computers unconstitutional. (Virginia case allows software filters on only some terminals). School Library Journal, vol. 45, p.17.

8. Goldberg, Beverly (1999, May). Internet watchdogs blast overreach of SmartFilter. (content blocking software). American Libraries, vol. 30, p.18.

9. Kniffel, Leonard (1996, May). Beijing determined to censor outside voices—on and off the 'Net. (Internet censorship in China). American Libraries, vol. 27, p. 28.

10. James Q. Wilson-Bureaucracy: What Government Agencies Do and Why They Do It-First Edition-2000

11. Lewyn, Mark (1989, December 4). Hackers: is a cure worse than the disease ? (blocking their mischief could mean crippling computer networks). Business Week, p. 37.

12. McCullagh, Declan (1996, August 7). China taking lessons from Singapore. McCullagh, Declan (1996, August 1). Internet Censorship.

13. Richard Stillman II—The American Bureaucracy, The Core of Modern Government. Second Edition-1996

14. Steven W. Hays and Richard C. Kearney-Public Personnel Administration-Problems and Prospects-third Edition-1995

15. Oumarou, Seydou Amadou and Rene Lefort (1998, September). The web, the spider and the fly. UNESCO-Courier, p. 38.

16. White, Cheryl and Heather Moors Johnson (1997, March). My son built a bomb (bomb-building information found on Internet). Ladies Home Journal, vol.114, p. 36.

17. Williams, Martyn (1999, August 9). Reporters Sans Frontieres Uncovers Enemies Of The Internet. Newsbytes News Network, p. PG.

18. W. Kip Viscusi, John M. Vernon, Joseph E. Harrington, Jr-Economics of Regulation and Antitrust-Second Edition-1995